STONE WALLS NOT A PRISON MAKE

STONE WALLS NOT A PRISON MAKE

The Anatomy of Planned Administrative Change

By

JOSEPH W. EATON

Professor of Social Work Research and Sociology
University of Pittsburgh
Pittsburgh, Pennsylvania

CHARLES C THOMAS • PUBLISHER

Springfield · Illinois · U.S.A.

Published and Distributed Throughout the World by

CHARLES C THOMAS · PUBLISHER

BANNERSTONE HOUSE

301-327 East Lawrence Avenue, Springfield, Illinois, U.S.A.

*With THOMAS BOOKS careful attention is given to all details of
manufacturing and design. It is the Publisher's desire to present books
that are satisfactory as to their physical qualities and artistic possibilities
and appropriate for their particular use. THOMAS BOOKS will be true
to those laws of quality that assure a good name and good will.*

To the memory of my mother and father

Flora and Jacob

INTRODUCTION

THE SCIENTIFIC SOCIAL MOVEMENT THEORY

This book deals with patterns of planned administrative change in a world behind bars. Bars securely shut-in those who have been committed there by society. Bars also serve to keep out the rest of us, although what happens there is of concern to the society that maintains them. What goes on behind bars is a reflection of a complex network of beliefs, expectations, and rules within which public officials conduct a job of awesome responsibility: the planning in minute detail of a total social system, where men who are their dependents spend every moment of many years of life.

Prisons are islands of social interaction in which administrative planning aims to exercise what approximates absolute control of inmates in order to accomplish several socially sanctioned purposes. Those who are responsible for the total planning often run institutions that violate many of the objectives for which society sanctions the institutions. Contradictions about what society expects from prisons must be resolved one way or the other by administrators. Intolerable conditions for inmates may develop as administrators combine their personal preferences with the social expectation that prisons safeguard society from offenders, punish them for their crime and keep prison costs low. Abusive tendencies are counteracted by the social expectation that prisons show compassion toward offenders and bring about their reform.

Reorientation programs have relied on three principal change techniques: religion, education and therapy. They have several attributes in common:

1. They aim to remake man.
2. They provide a rationale to bring about change by the application of a set of theoretical assumptions.
3. Each approach has a socially recognized identity expressed

in written formulations, organizations to espouse them, and leaders to advance their acceptance.

But here the similarity ends.

Religion postulates eternal values that become more cherished with age. They may be re-interpreted by each generation, but the old, not the new, is the source of confirmation. In contrast, education and therapy are change-oriented. While they also build on ideas first pronounced by great leaders, they accept the scientific creed which makes all knowledge subject to revision by added knowledge. Science, not faith, is the ultimate test of verity of the assertions of educators and therapists.

This book differs from many that have been written about prisons in its primary emphasis on the men who are expected to run them—prison officials and their staffs. In theory, the staff has almost absolute control over the inmates. Actually inmates often exercise considerable informal influence on their own living conditions, but prison officials retain final responsibility to accomplish re-socialization objectives that are widely shared throughout the United States and much of the world. Prisons are administered within the context of carefully formulated beliefs, accepted by the correctional movement. This social movement, largely composed of public employees, will be described and analyzed with recognition of the possibility that it illustrates patterns of planned administrative control and change of more generalized applicability.

Prison administrators, like all officials who are self-conscious change agents, work within a modern world where traditional doctrines are often questioned. Old doctrines tend to be replaced by new dogmas that claim science as their base, but retain many essentially ideological manifestations. The product of this organized effort to combine rational formulations with culturally sanctioned purposes results in what might be designated as a scientific social movement. It aims to apply scientific knowledge to the control of some aspects of human affairs. It is a hybrid with normative assumptions, social expectations, and organizational preferences by means of which administrators justify their plans to accomplish designated objectives.

This book addresses itself to the general question of how social programs are validated. It documents that administrators employ a process of *social* validation when, in the absence of sufficient scientific evidence to plan a program, they must make decisions as "best they can." They combine a little knowledge with a lot of guessing. They validate it for themselves by psychologically substituting their aspirations for evidence of accomplishment. They take encouragement from identifying with a scientific social movement which endows its program with the uncertain proof of plausibility; that an idea which enjoys popularity is more likely to be valid than one that is not?

No new idea can be developed and tried out with sufficient extensiveness to be tested for its effectiveness without some kind of social support. Scientists are also a part of our culture. They prefer to examine what they do by means of scientific methods. In this way they differ somewhat from the more common human trend to make the world seem as we want it to be. But devotion to absolute "truth" is not independent from social constraints. The history of science cannot be understood without viewing scientists in a social movement context. Prison reform in Calfornia is a case history that will be used to document this generalization.

ACKNOWLEDGMENTS

This book is the outcome of a venture of learning and research that began in August, 1956, when I joined the faculty of the University of California. Among my academic responsibilities was the making of a management survey of correctional research. Its aim was to increase the resources to be devoted to such research in California's crime control agencies and in the universities. I was given an identity card (with fingerprints) to get in and out of prison doors and carte blanche in deciding how to proceed. The survey was a cooperatively sponsored understaking of Donald S. Howard, Dean of the School of Social Welfare of the University of California at Los Angeles, and Richard A. McGee, Chairman of the Board of Corrections and Director of the Department of Corrections.

Over the years, funds or facilities for this study were provided by the National Institute of Mental Health, the California Department of Corrections, the University of California, and the University of Pittsburgh. Deans Wilber I. Newstetter of the Graduate School of Social Work at the University of Pittsburgh and Lenor S. Goerke of the School of Public Health at the University of California took more than a routine interest in the research. They were creative catalysts, helping to overcome administrative obstacles that have been the undoing of many a research project in an organization man era. The computing centers of both the University of California and the University of Pittsburgh made possible a rapid compilation of information that was unthinkable only two decades ago when I began my professional career.

This study combines historical, social-anthropological, and questionnaire data. The evidence used is both variable and uneven. The historical survey of the correctional movement was based entirely on secondary information. Social-anthropological data were obtained through occasional field visits and many opportunities to be a participant-observer in California state correctional activities, as research consultant to the Board of Corrections, member of the Citizen's Advisory Committee on Crime Prevention of the Attorney General, and member of the Board of Corrections' Research Advisory Board. The intensity is obviously limited with which so vast an administrative network as California's correctional agencies could be studied by one man, on a part-time basis. The task would have been completely unmanageable without the delightful intellectual comradeship of hundreds of unnamed men and women who have made correctional reform the object of their professional lives.

This book deals with the planning process in an organization that was willing to be identified. Much of the meaning of this case study for correctional specialists and the general public would have been lost had it been necessary to disguise the locale and the people involved. But in order to protect the feelings and organizational utility of many persons engaged in activities which they or the general reader might regard negatively, I have avoided reference to certain details or persons identified with them. The issues under consideration are not a matter of praise or blame. The concern is with understanding a sequence of events for its possible meaning for other similar social movements.

To Milton Burdman and J. Douglas Grant I feel very indebted. They not only served as liaison between the Department of Corrections and this study. They also greatly contributed to its scope and design. They, along with Norman Fenton, John Conrad, Winslow Rouse, Ronald Beatty, A. Lamont Smith, Robert Harrison, and Marie Veda Ryan, critically commented on parts or all of the manuscript in one or more of its several drafts. They served as key informants, teachers, collaborators, and devil's advocate. With candor rare among bureaucrats, they freely shared their own experiences and knowledge with me. Errors that remain in this volume are there in spite of their efforts to keep them out. They are my exclusive responsibility.

Information regarding the attitudes and background of correctional personnel was based on a survey of all of the employees made in January, 1959. Since 94 per cent of them responded with sufficiently complete questionnaires to be useable, our questionnaire data are based on what is close to a total sample of the total pertinent population. Its design, execution, and tabulation were a collaborative effort with a staff of social scientists of diverse talents. They included Professors Walter C. Bailey, Alfred H. Katz, and Alex Rosen, with later help from William Kennedy, Otto von Mering, and Kenneth Polk.

Other statistical information was furnished by the research staff or administrative officials of the agencies involved, particularly the Department of Corrections and the Bureau of Criminal Statistics. On many occasions the research apparatus of the Department of Corrections was placed at the disposal of this study to provide information that could not have been obtained otherwise. For instance, the distribution of the nearly 4,000 questionnaires to departmental personnel were in the hands of the Department's training officers Jack Stewart, Ray Morriston, Clark Cheff, E. E. Ayers, Bill Schneider, E. Brawley, Tom Murray, Harry Witek, Hazel Carlson and Clem Rice, under the coordination of Ray Procunier.

This book is in part an account of contemporary history. It could not rely exclusively on data in existing records and books. Much of the information came from lengthy interviews with participants at policy-making levels. I am particularly indebted for data to interviews with James Bennett, Director of the Federal Bureau of Prisons; E. R. Cass, Executive Secretary of the American Correctional Association; Dr. Milton Chernin, Dean of the School of Social Welfare at the University of California at Berkeley; the late Honorable Judge Burdette E. Daniels, Los Angeles; Walter Dunbar, Deputy Director and later Director of the Department of Corrections; Dr. Norman Fenton, the former Deputy Director of the Department of Corrections for Classification and Treatment and currently Director of the County Project in Correctional Methods; Richard Graves of Philadelphia; Karl Holton, the Probation Officer of Los Angeles County; Richard A. McGee, Director of the Department of Correction and more recently Agency Administrator of Correctional Services in the State of California; Professor Austin H. MacCormick of the University of California and Osborne Association; Judge Isaac Pacht of Los Angeles; Professor Thorsten

Sellin of the Department of Sociology at the University of Pennsylvania; Heman Stark, Director of the Department of the Youth Authority; Chief Justice Earl Warren, Washington, D. C., and Judge Albert C. Wollenberg of San Francisco.

I was fortunate in having the able assistance of Hilda M. Reitzel and Helen-Jean Moore preparing the manuscript for the printer. They made many valuable editorial suggestions. The charts are the artistic production of Stephan Shapiro. Allan R. Ottley of the California State Library searched its files for background data about the Rev. James Woodworth, who represented California at the first American Prison Congress in Cincinnati in 1870. Carl Girshman called my attention to Richard Lovelace's poem "To Althea, From Prison" (1642) which inspired part of the title of this book.

Over the years the study had several full-time and part-time secretaries and research assistants who coded schedules and prepared manuscript copy and related documents. Edna Anish, Carol Cappell, Barbara Caputo, Shirley Corsin, Lila Goodman, Betty Gunderson, Margaret Hansen, Alice L. Harper, Sylvia Khan, Trudi Leipzig, Donna Mandell, Helen Phelps, Bonnie Simpson, and Sue Wilcox deserve a place in this acknowledgment, not as a matter of form but because they became interested in the substance of this study. They approached their tasks with more than ordinary concern.

Social research, like most research, is a risk venture. It begins without assurance of a completed product. There is no certainty that results will justify the efforts of the many who worked together to make this study possible. In sustaining my perspective and enthusiasm for this venture, my wife, Helen, did far more than she realizes.

J.W.E.

CONTENTS

TABLES

CHARTS

STONE WALLS NOT A PRISON MAKE

Chapter 1

THE CORRECTIONAL MOVEMENT

Throughout human history, offenders against their society's laws have often been sinned against by those charged with law enforcement. Oppressive state actions to make men conform were a major issue in the American Revolution. Concern for individual rights, even those of criminals, is woven into the United States Constitution. It provides for trial by jury and prohibits conviction without reasonable grounds. Excessive bail, or fines, cruel and unusual punishment are also proscribed. Similar protective clauses are contained in most of the state constitutions.

State action to remake deviant citizens has often failed to conform to these constitutional ideals. When a French survey team came to the United States in 1831 to study democratic crime control methods, the team members were shocked. August de Beaumont and Alexis de Tocqueville reported, for instance, that in "Ohio, which possesses a penal code remarkable for the mildness and humanity of its provisions, the prisons were barbarous. We have deeply sighed, when at Cincinnati visiting the prison, we found half of the imprisoned chained with irons and the rest plunged into an infected dungeon. We are unable to describe the painful impression which we experienced when, examining the prison of New Orleans, we found men together with hogs, in the midst of all odors and nuisances. In locking up the criminals, nobody thinks of rendering them better, but only of taming their malice; they are put in chains like ferocious beasts, and instead of being corrected, they are rendered brutal."[1]

This is how they summed up their impression: "While society

---

[1]Gustave August de Beaumont and Alexis de Tocqueville: *On the Penitentiary System in the United States and Its Application in France.* Philadelphia, Carey, Lea and Blanchard, 1833, trans. Dr. Francis Lieber.

3

in the United States gives the example of the most extended liberty, the prisons of the same country offer the spectacle of the most complete despotism."[1]

CORRECTIONAL REFORM

Inconsistency between ideals avowed by enlightened leaders and the actions of those charged with direct responsibility for prisoners gives rise to correctional reform: The substitution of the principle of correction for retribution; preference for the use of intelligence rather than force; treatment in lieu of punishment; and the testing by research, rather than by their popularity, of the consequences of particular correctional practices.

Correctional reform is as ancient as organized punishment. When the Hebrews adopted a code of laws, it contained the well-known injunction, "An eye for an eye and a tooth for a tooth." It aimed to limit revenge and keep punishment from being far more extensive than the crime. In every part of the globe there have been men who advocated compassion for the criminal. A few are remembered because, through the forces of their personality and a gifted pen, they have had a lasting impact on the evolution of correctional reform. Among them were Cesare Bonesana Beccaria, Voltaire, and Jeremy Bentham, whose appeal to the conscience and the sense of the practical of their contemporaries helped to nurture a critical review of penal practices in the dawn of our modern era.[2]

Prison reform became an international cause through the travels and personal crusade of John Howard. He was born in 1726 in England to wealth and used it to pursue social reform ideals. He introduced many social-economic reforms on his estate, including the provision of schools for the children of his tenants. In 1756 he was elected a Fellow of the Royal Society as a "true lover of natural philosophy."[3] In that year, after an earthquake that

---

[1]*Ibid.*: 47.

[2]Marcello T. Maestro: *Voltaire and Beccaria as Reformers of the Criminal Law.* New York, Columbia University Press, 1942; Cesare Bonesana Beccaria: *Essays on Crimes and Punishments.* With a commentary attributed to M. de Voltaire. New York, Little, 1924; *The Works of Jeremy Bentham.* Edinburgh, William Tait, 1843, Vol. I.

[3]Max Grünhutt: *Renal Reform: A Comparative Study.* Oxford, The Clarendon Press, 1948.

nearly destroyed Lisbon, Howard decided to travel there in order to help the survivors. Enroute, he had his first experience with prisons, to the reform of which he became dedicated in the autumn of his life. The British ship on which he travelled was captured by privateers en route to Lisbon. He and other passengers were turned over to the French at Brest. Since France was then at war with England, John Howard was "confined in a dungeon, dark, damp and filthy beyond description."[1] Punishment and control were then the only objectives of prison management. Little thought was given to the objective remaking of criminals into citizens who could live as free men among their fellow citizens.

Nearly twenty years later, in 1773, John Howard was appointed Sheriff of Bedford. Unlike most of his gentlemanly predecessors, he took more than symbolic interest in this post. Moved by the many abuses which he found, he became a reformer. He was particularly incensed by the practice of keeping innocent men, or those whose sentence had expired, in prison for non-payment of their lodgings to the gaolkeeper, who was entitled to collect fees from inmates. He asked the justices of the peace for intervention, but they declined for lack of a precedent. In search of this, he went on the first of his many prison tours, which took him all over England, Europe, and the Middle East to inspect prisons and hospitals and to plead the cause of more humane care of institutionalized persons. He carefully documented his findings in one of the first empirical social research surveys of the modern era.[2] Howard's effective advocacy of prison reform made him a citizen of the world by the time of his death in 1790.

Howard's crusade inspired others, particularly in the United States. Concern for human rights was high in the former British colonies, whose inhabitants had rebelled against the mother country under the banner of human rights. In Pennsylvania, where the

---

[1] Hepworth Dixon: *John Howard and the Prison World of Europe.* Webster, Massachusetts, Frederick Charlton, Publisher, 1852.

[2] John Howard: *The State of the Prisons in England and Wales, with Preliminary Observations and an Account of Some Foreign Prisons and Hospitals.* Warrington, England, William Eyries, Printer, 1777; also *An Account of the Principal Lazarettos in Europe with Various Papers Relative to the Plaque: Together with Further Observations on Some Foreign Prisons and Hospitals.* Warrington, England, William Eyries, Printer, 1789.

Quakers had much influence, penal reform was legislated during the first year of independence. A constitution was adopted with the provision that the legislature proceed, "as soon as might be, to the reform of the penal laws, and invent punishments less sanguinary and better proportioned to the various degree of criminality."[1] Quaker religious doctrines were fundamentally opposed to the vengeful spirit of the British penal code, which specified the death penalty for an increasing variety of offenses until the list contained 222 during the 18th Century.[2]

Penal reform sentiments in Pennsylvania were influenced by John Howard,[3] but they also had native roots. William Penn, the colony's founder in 1682, had personally experienced the indignities and horrors of British prisons where he spent six months for refusal to take an oath. When he and other Quakers arrived in America, they adopted a humanitarian criminal code which contrasted greatly with prevailing practices elsewhere. The new code abolished most categories of religious offenses that existed in English law. It relied far more on imprisonment and restitution of damages to the victims to control crime than on the death penalty. This Quaker penal code remained in effect until 1718, when the more punitive English pattern was adopted and the death penalty could again be imposed for thirteen offenses, including witchcraft. Cruel and unusual punishment became increasingly prevalent in Pennsylvania, as in the other English colonies, although such practices never were so widespread as in the English mother-country and in Europe.

Penal reform became more than a personal crusade, when in 1787, a number of citizens of Philadelphia (most of them Quakers) organized under the appropriate name of the Society for Alleviating the Miseries of Public Prisons. Its Secretary, Caleb Lownes, with the support of such prominent leaders as Benjamin Rush, Benjamin Franklin, and William Bradford, lobbied actively and

---

[1]Orlando F. Lewis: *The Development of American Prisons and Prison Customs, 1776 to 1845, with Special Reference to Early Institutions in the State of New York.* New York, printed by the Prison Association of New York, 1922.

[2]E. C. Wines: *The State of Prisons and of Child-saving Institutions in the Civilized World.* Cambridge, Mass., University Press, 1880.

[3]Negley K. Teeters: *They Were in Prison, A History of the Philadelphia Prison Society.* Philadelphia, John C. Winston Co., 1937.

successfully for abolition of the barbarous colonial criminal code.[1]
Between 1770 and 1776, there were several deaths from starvation
in the jail, and prisoners were in many cases "almost entirely without clothing or bedding."[2] There was no separation of prisoners
by sex. The keeper's practice of sometimes locking up male and
female prisoners in the same room resulted in debauchery repugnant to many. The Society was instrumental in getting support for
the building of a new type of prison on Walnut Street, America's
first reform installation. It had sixteen solitary cells, with separate
quarters for the detention of suspects, witnesses, and misdemean-
ants. It was possible for inmates to work and to be released before
the end of their terms if an investigation revealed that they had
reformed. No irons or chains were allowed. Guards were forbidden
to use sabres or canes.

The new humane approach was credited with a reduction of
crime. Prison commitments dropped from 131 in 1789 to 45 in
1893. Four years before the Walnut Street Prison was opened there
were 104 prisoner escapes. Not one escaped during the first four
years of the new facility, except fourteen inmates who ran away on
the opening day as part of a plot to discredit the innovation engi-
neered by the hostile jailer.

Initial enthusiasm for the Walnut Street Prison shortly gave
way to disillusionment. Its facilities became overcrowded by the
turn of the century. It became harder to maintain good sanitary
conditions. An epidemic of jail fever broke out in 1802. The industrial work program for inmates was discontinued. Laxity, favor-
itism, and politics became characteristic of its administration.[3] A

1On March 9, 1787, Benjamin Rush read a paper to a group of intellectuals, who
met at the home of Benjamin Franklin, on "An Enquiry Into the Effects of Public
Punishment Upon Criminals and Upon Society." He advocated that the only purpose
of punishment was the reformation of the criminal. Ten years later, Rush publicly
attacked the use of the death penalty in his "An Enquiry Into the Consistency of
Punishment of Murder by Death with Reason and Revelation." These papers were
published as pamphlets. See Nathan G. Goodman, *Benjamin Rush, Physician and
Citizen, 1746-1813*. Philadelphia, The University of Pennsylvania Press, 1934.

2Albert G. Fraser: "The Function of a Prison Society in a Penological Program."
Proceedings, 62nd Annual Congress of the American Prison Association, New York,
1932.

3Orlando F. Lewis: *Op. Cit.:* 38-42.

cycle of correctional reform had taken a course to be repeated many times. A step forward would be succeeded by backsliding.

During the 19th Century, the correctional field was vitalized by highly personalized conflict of theories. The Pennsylvania Prisons Society advocated the incarceration of inmates in solitary confinement, to encourage the doing of penitence. Human contacts were restricted to prison employees, visitors from the Prison Society, and ministers. Separation of inmates in individual cells was advocated as a pre-requisite for individualized treatment.

This theory of management was opposed by one in which inmates would be allowed to congregate during the day, to perform useful labor, but under conditions of strict silence. It became known as the Auburn System, named after the prison in New York State in which the idea was first applied. Its principal and sometimes acrimonious advocate was Lewis Dwight, whose interest in prisons began when, as an agent of the American Society, he distributed Bibles to inmates of jails and prisons. Like John Howard, Dwight was motivated to become a crusader by personal experience with the sight of prison degradation and misery. The Boston Prison Discipline Society, which influenced American penology in many ways, was largely his personal creation. It died with him in 1854.[1]

The questions at issue in this historic controversy apply to this day. Solitary and separate confinement continue to be used, sometimes as a form of punishment, more often as a means of control of dangerous criminals, and on occasions as a temporary measure to help an inmate gain control of himself. Most prisoners, however, are brought together for work, meals, and recreational activities. Silence is no longer imposed.

Neither the Pennsylvania nor the Auburn system has won out. Reformers reject both on humanitarian grounds. But the controversy had at least this function for the development of penology. The supporters of both schools of thought made polemic use of data to support their contentions. They were in agreement that for intelligent policy-making in correctional affairs more than religiously motivated compassion and concern for human rights were

---

[1]Blake McKelvey: *American Prisons: A Study of American Social History Prior to 1915*. Chicago, Illinois, The University of Chicago Press, 1936.

required. Scientific evidence regarding the consequences of one or the other system of management would have to be looked at.

The controversy was often vitriolic because correctional reform was highly personalized. Facts were used as weapons by crusaders with convictions. But, in their battle for support from uncommitted penologists, they had to rely on evidence to support their ideas. They called attention to starvation of prisoners, calculated neglect, the general desirability of abolishing corporal punishment, torture, imprisonment for debt, and other practices that were in conflict with the humanistic philosophy that swelled in the nineteenth century.

The reformers of the 19th Century advocated most of the ideas of prisoner treatment that still are regarded by some as too soft and progressive. No individual or small group of citizens could for very long overcome the lethargy of legislators and the usual administrative careerists. Before a national reform policy could emerge, there had to be an ideologically rooted program supported by more broadly based groups than a handful of well-intentioned philanthropists.

A NATIONAL ORGANIZATION EMERGES

A pivotal event in the history of correctional reform occurred in Cincinnati, Ohio, during the week of October 12, 1870. Penologists from twenty-five states, the Republic of Colombia, and Canada, met to found the National Prison Association. Its first Congress was attended not only by reformers, but also by many state officials, wardens, and politicians who had direct responsibility for the administration of their state prisons.

This meeting was organized by one of America's least recognized social welfare scholars and organizers, Enoch Cobb Wines. At the age of fifty-six, after more than thirty years in the field of education, biblical-classical scholarship, and the ministry, he accepted the post of Secretary of the Prison Association of New York in 1862. Within a few years it became an organization of more than local significance. By 1870, contributions came from humanist reformers from many parts of the country and the world. For instance, among the life patrons, who contributed $500 at one time, were John Stuart Mill, M.P. in England; Dr. Francis Lieber, Professor of Political Science at Columbia College in New York; Miss Dorothea Dix, Boston, Massachusetts; and Miss Florence Nightingale of London. From its inception, until the present, the New York Society has provided staff and space for the National Prison Association and contributes to its annual budget.

The correctional movement emerged in an era when humanist sentiment and an interest in a scientific approach to man were in ascendancy. The idea that man could plan his own future shaped human endeavors in education, in public welfare, and child care, in work with the mentally ill and the mentally retarded, in movements affecting working conditions, and in governmental affairs. Wines worked closely with leaders of the American Social Science Association where men of science and philanthropists met to exchange ideas and debate their divergencies. This movement, organized after the Civil War in 1865, gave birth to the American Sociological Association, the American Economic Association, the American Political Science Association, and the National Conference of Social Welfare. It emerged within the same cultural ferment as the American Correctional movement.[1]

Enoch Cobb Wines went beyond advocating reform ideas then in vogue. He initiated a thorough survey of prisons and reformatories in eighteen eastern states. Along with Theodore William Dwight, a professor of law at Columbia University, Wines inspected many prisons and discovered conditions of extreme overcrowding and mal-administration. The study also covered policy issues like the question of classification of inmates, as well as minute management problems like the frequency of laundering the prisoner clothes. Their research was similar in many respects to the surveys of John Howard, made seventy to eighty years earlier. But even more than his predecessor, Enoch Cobb Wines abstracted policy generalizations from his data. He agitated for an organized, rather than a personal approach to prison reform in accordance with the

---

[1]L. L. Bernard and Jessie Bernard: *Origins of American Sociology, The Social Science Movement in the United States*. New York, Thomas Y. Crowell Company, 1943; F. B. Sanborn: "E. C. Wines and Prison Reform," in Charles R. Henderson, *Correction and Prevention*. New York, Russell Sage Foundation, 1910.

principle that the remaking of criminals, not the infliction of suffering, is the primary objective of incarceration.[1]

Wines was instrumental in arousing nationwide interest in a national congress of penologists. His friend, F. B. Sanborn, Executive Secretary of the American Social Science Association, helped to elicit support from its members all over the country. All persons interested in prisons and prisoners could join. Prison reform was a cause which appealed to the general optimism of intellectuals during an era when they first believed that science could be used to plan a more perfect society.

ADOPTION OF AN IDEOLOGY

The first national prison congress in 1870 attracted lay persons as well as professionals, wardens, educators, pastors, and philanthropists. Rutherford B. Hayes, then the Governor of Ohio, agreed to serve as Conference Chairman. Enoch Wines set the tone of the deliberation in a speech asserting that "the students of penitentiary science, the workers in the field of penitentiary discipline in this country, have come to a substantial agreement on certain fundamental principles of criminal treatment and approaching such agreement in others. What are these great principles, these moral citadels around which the din of battle is either wholly ceased, or is year by year, becoming more and more feeble?" They included advocacy of the following ideas:[2]

1. The primary aim of public punishment is the protection of society against criminals through the reformation of the transgressor.

2. The principle of progressive classification should be applied to all.

3. The principle of reward and inducement to good conduct and reformation should be applied in prison administration, with indeterminate sentences to make punishment

---

[1]Enoch Cobb Wines and Theodore William Dwight: "Report on the Prisons and Reformatories of the United States and Canada," in Prison Association of New York, *Twenty-third Annual Report.* Albany, New York, The Argus Company, 1868.

[2]Prison Association of New York, "Transactions of the National Congress on Penitentiary and Reformatory Discipline," *Twenty-sixth Annual Report of the Executive Committee, for the Year 1870.* Albany, New York, 1871.

fit the criminal not only the crime.
4. Probation should be used in the place of imprisonment.
5. Religion and education should be utilized in prison pro-
    grams.
6. Prisoners should be employed in useful labor.
7. Imprisonment should be continued until reformation is
    affected.
8. Political control of prisons should be eliminated.
9. Preventive institutions should be developed.
10. Prisons should be staffed with professionally qualified
    officers.

These policy recommendations reflected the consensus of reform penologists. A few, like Warden Zebulon R. Brockway of the
Detroit House of Correction, were trying to apply them, but most
of the prison officials who voted for the adoption of this program
only paid lip service to it.

Zebulon R. Brockway, Superintendent of the Detroit House of
Corrections and the man who set up reform precedents for a quarter
of a century as first Superintendent of America's pioneer reformatory at Elmira, New York, read a paper on the "Ideal of a True
Prison System for a State."[1] Brockway's well reasoned statement
reflected the consensus of reform penologists, but most of the prison
officials who voted for the *Declaration of Principles* grossly violated
them in their day-to-day work. They were ambivalent, if not
opposed, to its humanitarian spirit and its correctional principles.
Yet they voted for it. Blake McKelvey comments on this paradox
by calling attention to the fact that the convention was called by
reformers, who knew what they believed and had come with well
prepared speeches. The more traditional and punitively oriented
prison administrators had no equally effective spokesmen. They
had no ideology of their own to oppose the reformers:

> Overwhelmed with inspired addresses, prayers and song and
> much exhortation, even the hard-headed wardens were carried
> up for a mountain top experience. In their enthusiasm for the
> ideal, they arose above the monotony of four gray walls, men in
> stripes shuffling in lock steps, sullen faces staring through bars,
> coarse mush and coffee made of bread crusts, armed sentries stalk-

[1]*Ibid.*: 38-65.

ing the walls. They forgot it all and voted for their remarkable declaration of principles. Society is responsible for the reformation of criminals; education, religion and industrial training are valuable aids in this undertaking; discipline should build rather than destroy the self-respect of each prisoner; his cooperation can best be secured with an indeterminate sentence under which his discharge is regulated by a merit system; the responsibility of the state extends into the field of preventive institutions and to the aid and supervision of prisoners after discharge; a central state control should be established so as to secure a stable, non-political administration, trained officers and reliable statistics.[1]

It is probably significant that the organized correctional movement in America began with a written platform, although it did not become a program of aggressive social action. The *Declaration of Principles* never was more than an expression of ideological direction. In the extensive penal reform effort of California, to be described later in this book, no explicit reference is made to the *Principles* in that Department's in-service training literature, although what is happening there conforms to this *Declaration*. It is a moral creed, with considerable symbolic significance. Like the platform of any of America's political parties, the *Declaration of Principles* represented ideals to which leaders paid lip service at the very least. It represented a common core of beliefs, from which actual practice deviates. It served as a common reference point and an ideological stabilizer of successive generations of leaders in the correctional field.

In 1930, at its convention in St. Louis, the American Prison Association re-affirmed the *Declaration of Principles* with slight alterations. Dr. Hastings H. Hart, who rose to second the motion to re-affirm the *Declaration* to have it read each year, and to have it printed in each year's *Proceedings,* did so with the following comment regarding the *Declaration's* importance:

It is to my mind a most remarkable thing that this Declaration was written sixty years ago at the very start of the American Prison Association. We have had annual discussions for sixty years. At the end of forty-nine years, this Association added two points, and then again we are adding three more points to the original declaration.

---

[1]Blake McKelvey: *American Prisons:* 71.

We added the individual study and treatment of the criminal. We have added probation and parole, and we have added the matter of uniform statistics.

The genius that conceived this was tremendous. Think of it. After sixty years of discussion, we find only these minor changes can be made in that great *Declaration*.[1]

Correctional reformers and status quo prison officials had been amalgamated by Enoch Wines. He served as their ideological and administrative catalyst. Most of them were administrators, who were working for more than a paycheck. Their work became a cause in which they invested of themselves. But their movement quickly lost momentum when left without Wines: active leadership. Correctional reform had no mass support. It was dependent for its survival, as are all social movements in their infancy, on a small cadre of enthusiasts.

In 1874, the National Prison Association lacked sufficient funds to print the *Proceedings* of its St. Louis gathering. The New York Association, whose budget then as now subsidized the national efforts, was able to continue only after a severe retrenchment of its activities. No national congresses took place between 1876 and 1882. In the following year, W. M. F. Round, Secretary of the New York Prison Association, and Franklin Sanborn, President of the American Social Science Association, were barely able to assemble a quorum of five members, to re-elect ex-President Rutherford B. Hayes as head of the reconstituted National Prison Association. He served in this formal role until the year of his death in 1893.[2] His prestige and personality helped to keep within the same fold reform oriented penologists and the more custody-oriented wardens, who did not feel comfortable in their association with the former.

---

[1]American Prison Association, *Proceedings of the Sixtieth Annual Congress of the American Prison Association*. New York, 1930.

[2]W. M. F. Round: "General Rutherford B. Hayes," in Charles R. Henderson (ed.), *Correction and Prevention*. New York, Russell Sage Foundation, 1910; Round reported that he had to hunt up one person in a Saratoga boarding house just recovering from a severe illness. He agreed to come to the meeting to make a quorum "at great risk to his health."

ORGANIZATION + IDEOLOGY = A SOCIAL MOVEMENT

The organization survived. In 1908 its name was changed to *American Prison Association* and in 1955 to *American Correctional Association*.[1] For many years it did nothing more than to sponsor an annual meeting of American prison officials and on occasion to sponsor technical working committees. Throughout this period, they continued to pay lip-service to their *Declaration of Principles* which was brought up to date in 1930, 1950 and, most recently in 1960.[2] And there always were people who wanted to implement the principles. Their speeches advocated a policy of substitution of chains and other physical restraints by human intelligence and rehabilitation. But their ideological leadership did not produce organizational control. Many of the working committees of the American Correctional Association were dominated by wardens who generally were punitive and traditionalistic in their outlook. They were highly responsive to pressures from influential citizens, newspaper editors and public officials who often were vociferous in stressing that justice and wisdom are best served by "tough" prisons. The *Declaration of Principles* as a creed was and still is inconsistent with the way offenders are being treated in many state prisons, and in most county and city jails.

Contradictions between ideology and action are common in human affairs. The Ten Commandments have never described the actual morality of the many populations who have espoused them. The American Declaration of Independence and Constitutions co-exist with systematic denial to Negroes of their constitutionally guaranteed rights.

In spite of these contradictions, the adoption of a credo by the first national meeting of prison officials in 1870 cannot be dismissed as irrelevant to the history of prison reform. The American Correctional Association stood for ideals that were perceived by its members as being "higher" than those they could live by in their day-to-day job. The code brought together persons that were

---

[1] Peter P. Lejins: "Penal Reform in the American Correctional Association," Prison Association of New York, *The One Hundred and Thirteenth Annual Report of the Prison Associaiton of New York, 1957.*

[2] See Appendix for a copy of the 1960 version.

part of a professional reference group, people with common tasks, questions, over-lapping career lines, and similar occupational status. The road to respectability and recognition in this reference group of prison officials required at least lip-service to the goal of changing penal practices to conform with correctional reform standards. Its principles thus served to counteract tendencies in prisons to condone cruelty, neglect, and vengeance. They have supported efforts to try out new techniques for motivating prisoners to live up to society's expectations.

THE MOVEMENT'S INTERNATIONAL ARENA

The correctional movement had international scope from its very inception. Since John Howard's day, prison reformers all over the world have communicated with one another. Humanitarian programs in one country have been studied by like-minded persons elsewhere. The first international congress convened in Frankfort-on-the-Main in 1846, at the initiative of the Inspector Generals of prisons in Belgium and England. Other meetings followed in Brussels in 1847 and again in Frankfort in 1857.[1]

After the organization of the first American Prison Congress in 1870, Enoch C. Wines set out to elicit international support of the principles it had adopted. He induced the United States Congress to appropriate $5,000 to implement this resolution by inviting the nations of the world to send delegates to a truly international congress of prison reform. In order to accept an appointment as United States Commissioner, he resigned from his post as Secretary of the Prison Association of New York. In his new capacity, he could expand his reform concerns to cover the world.

Largely as a result of his catalytic efforts, about four hundred representatives from twenty-two nations met in July, 1872. In addressing the congress, Wines expressed the hope the delegates had "come together to give shape, point, and practical force to a

[1]For details, see Martino Beltrani Scalia, "Historical Sketch of National and International Penitentiary Conferences in Europe and America," Prison Association of New York, *Twenty-sixth Annual Report.* Albany, The Argus Company, 1871; Enoch C. Wines, *The State of Prisons and Child-saving Institutions in the Civilized World.* Cambridge, Massachusetts, University Press, John Wilson and Company, __?__.

great movement in favor of penitentiary reform."[1] The conference expressed appreciation of the breadth and comprehensiveness of the declarations of its executive committee, which included propositions substantially like those of the *Declaration of Principles* adopted in Cincinnati, but no formal vote was taken. None of the delegates were empowered to speak for their governments. The International Penal and Penitentiary Commission was organized, with Wines as first Chairman. The Commission sponsored twelve international congresses[2] between 1872 and 1951, when it was dissolved because its functions were being performed by the United Nations Economic and Social Council.

The International Congresses were forums, not action groups. Like the American Correctional Association, they served as a periodic meeting ground in which policies and problems were discussed at a more idealistic level than consonant with the practices of any of the participating countries. They gave international recognition to reform elements in various countries through the weight of their discussions. The congresses often were preceded by systematic surveys of prison problems. Wines prepared an extensive factual survey of existing conditions and needed reforms all over the world on the basis of data collected in connection with the second congress in Stockholm in 1878.[3] In preparation for the eighth congress in Washington, D. C., in 1910, the American Prison Association and the Russell Sage Foundation sponsored an extensive survey of American penology and published a five volume work, copies of which were presented to each Delegate.[4]

The congresses served as platforms for informal and occasionally open criticism of penal practices in some of the larger countries

[1]Negley K. Teeters: *Deliberations of the International Penal and Penitentiary Congresses.* Philadelphia, Temple University Bookstore, 1949.

[2]International Penal and Penitentiary Commission, *Proceedings of the Session Held at Berne.* Berne, Switzerland, Staempfli Cie, 1951.

[3]Enoch C. Wines: *The State of Prisons and Child-saving Institutions in the Civilized World.* Wines did not live to see it published. He died suddenly in 1879, after writing the preface, in the midst of revising page proof.

[4]Charles R. Henderson (ed.): *Correction and Prevention Series* (New York, Russell Sage Foundation, 1910): Vol. I: "Prison Reform"; Vol. II: "Penal and Reformatory Institutions"; Vol. III: "Preventive Means"; Vol. IV: "The Love and Treatment of Children," ed. Hastings Hart and Thomas J. Homer; Vol. V: "Juvenile Court Laws in the United States."

that aspired to being recognized as "advanced." In Washington, the Czarist prison system was strongly condemned, particularly the practice of exiling political offenders in Siberia. A British delegate suggested, however, "that Americans were in no position to criticize Russia's penal treatment when, at that very moment (1910) many southern states were shackled with the 'chain-gang' with all its brutalities."[1] In 1935, when the congress met in Berlin, many of the international delegates expressed hostility toward the Nazi system of penal practices, particularly its concentration camps, whose brutal regulations were circulated to the delegates.[2]

The international prison congresses were without noticeable impact on the penal practices of member states. As in the American congresses, reform ideas dominated most of the deliberations. Discussants highlighted goals to be achieved. Lofty reform ideals were given the sanction of an international reference group of penal officials, but few immediate practical consequences resulted.

In 1955, the United Nations convened a Congress on the Prevention of Crime and Treatment of Offenders. It proposed detailed standards for minimum rules for the treatment of prisoners. After discussion, the rules were adopted by the Economic and Social Council, thus giving international sanction to a bill of rights for prisoners all over the world. The United Nations congress also adopted recommendations regarding the selection and training of personnel for penal and correctional institutions, but these were not formally adopted by the Economic and Social Council.[3]

Correctional reform ideals have attained international recognition, but they have never been the concern of a large number of persons. This fact may be related to the absence of an interested group of prison "alumni." Ex-inmates do not want to be reminded of their past. In this respect, they differ greatly from veterans, ex-mental patients, cripples, orphans, and other former inmates of total institutions,[4] who often strive hard to support the improve-

---

[1]Negley K. Teeter.: *Deliberations of the International Penal and Penitentiary Congresses.*

[2]*Ibid.*: 178.

[3]Prison Association of New York, *The One Hundred and Thirteenth Annual Report of the Prison Association of New York.* New York, 1957.

[4]The concept of total institution is the most appropriate analytic device for examining the structure and the functions of prisons. It stresses the features that prisons

ment of services. Prison reformers have been able to count on such general support only on rare occasions. Reform ideals are not the creed of a popular movement. They have remained a cause espoused largely by prison officials, who have on the whole avoided becoming generally identified with political movements which criticize existing institutions.

Penal reforms tend to be very circumscribed. They are not "packaged" with advocacy of general reforms of economic and social conditions, like unemployment and racial discrimination, which are definitely related to the incidence of certain types of crime. This conservative framework of prison reform has to be viewed within the context of the fact that all prison officials are government employees. Their influence and future career are dependent on acceptance by the political structure. Caution and patience have kept reform-oriented penologists from acting in full accordance of their convictions. Here and there individual leaders, who have enjoyed considerable public esteem, have been able to champion less popular causes such as the abolition of the death penalty or a less punitive approach to drug addicts. But, in general, correctional reform goals have been achieved through working without publicity to induce even very conservative elements to support at least a partial reform orientation. Gradualism, rather than urgency, has characterized the movement.

This gradualistic orientation precluded examination of unpopular policy alternatives that would be "too far out of line," with public opinion. Often it resulted in the substitution of talk for action. Even where correctional reform attained a high level of implementation one finds considerable ritualistic avowal of reform ideals that are reflected by only minor or no actual changes of programming.

The correctional movement thus avoided being designated as idealistic, too welfare oriented or too soft. But it also never lost its

---

have in common with other organizations where administrators are responsible for planning and managing the conditions of life of inmates, clients or volunteers, who not only work but live together under highly regulated conditions. Erving Goffman, "On the Characteristics of Total Institutions," *Proceedings of the Symposium on Preventive and Social Psychiatry*. Washington, D. C., Walter Reed Army Institute of Research, 1957.

concern for the adoption of more humane policies and more scientific procedures. The movement and its principles stand in dramatic contrast to the occasional advocacy of state sponsored abuses, tortures, and murders in the name of "national interest." The trial of Adolf Eichmann in Jerusalem in 1961 highlights the fact that political and ideological considerations can condone the employment of the most primitive penal abuses and cruelties, even in an age of modern technology. The establishment and maintenance of Nazi concentration and extermination camps was possible only because of the personal participation of hundreds of thousands of German civil servants, police officials, and soldiers, and their assistance by persons in every country which the Germans occupied.

The correctional reform movement led by prison officials holds up clearly contradictory standards. It acts as a social restraint against abuses that can and do develop when the state sanctions the use of force against an individual. It makes the plea that deviants, no matter how unpopular, must be dealt with in light of policies consistent with humanitarian principles and correctional procedures that can stand the test of being evaluated by their consequences for society as well as for prisoners.

SCIENCE AND THE SOCIAL MOVEMENT

Many social movements have remade their world. Some were primarily religious, like Mohammedanism, Lutheranism, Methodism, and more recently, Christian Science. Others were primarily political, the Nationalist movements of every land that had to fight for its freedom, Communism, Socialism or the Suffragette movement. Each movement was embodied in an organization with an ideology that was endowed with moral certainty. Its principles were viewed as being eternal in their verity, to be asserted and believed, not to be tested.

The correctional reform movement has something in common with these religious and political instruments of social change. It avows principles believed to rest on *a priori* ethical assertions, such as their general humanitarian orientation and belief in the dignity of human beings, even when the individuals have committed crimes. But the correctional movement has also been imbued with a belief in scientific rationalism. This fact differentiates it from religious and political movements. Its principles have been viewed as temporary rather than permanent, subject to proof and verification.

John Howard and Enoch Cobb Wines did more than advocate a point of view that they believed to be morally right. They studied prison conditions and accumulated evidence to prove that the conditions which they decried failed to accomplish the purposes for which they were sometimes defended: the protection of society and the reformation of the inmates.

From the very beginning of the American Correctional Association, scientifically oriented persons have played their parts. At the 1870 Congress, a committee on criminal statistics reported a plan for the systematic accumulation of data for the comparative study of penal problems.[1] Like most of the recommendations to the Congress, this one was not implemented, but the idea that science is pertinent to policy-making built into the correctional movement a mechanism for change. Right and wrong are not matters of ethical absolutism. They were from time to time decisively influenced by what was found to be empirically true or false.

Correctional reform had largely been a matter of lip-service in many places. Piece-meal reforms were initiated periodically all over the United States, often to be wiped out by bureaucratic realities such as staff changes which brought people into power who were neither enthusiastic nor interested in the innovations, shortage of funds, overcrowding of prisons, or too many of the other reasons that lead men to postpone until tomorrow actions they say they want to do today. That "tomorrow" somehow never arrived.

Extensive and widespread application of both the ideals and scientific aspirations of the correctional movement began in America in the 1920's with several important sociological and legal research studies and the organization in the 1930's of a unified Federal Bureau of Prisons. In the 1940's another ingredient was added to the correctional movement: long-range administrative planning. Fundamental reforms began to take organizational root in Califor-

---

[1] A. J. Curt: "Criminal Statistics," The Prison Association of New York, *Twenty-sixth Annual Report*.

nia and several other states, particularly Wisconsin, New Jersey, and Washington.

The administrative blueprints for correctional reform that were made living realities before and after World War II did not remain a matter of private know-how. They were compiled and published in 1954 by the American Correctional Association as a *Manual of Correctional Standards*.[1] The Manual recommended in detail methods of translating correctional ideals into reality. Shortly after its publication, members of the American Correctional Association could think of enough suggestions for improvement to warrant undertaking a comprehensive revision, which was published in 1959. Included were chapters on research and program evaluation, advocating that they become a regular organizational function.

The emergence of the correctional reform movement has been sketched briefly to identify the sequence of events by which it inspired the well-planned change of one entire state prison system— that of the State of California. What happened there is not unique. It has happened, and is happening, in many other states in America. Programs exist today in many localities to reduce the gap between the ideals of a correctional reform movement and the realities of prisons, jails, and other correctional institutions. The California story is worth telling, however, because it has implications for prison reform everywhere, to the extent that one can identify the administrative processes by which California's reform was achieved. The story illustrates what is administratively feasible, but also what obstacles emerge and what contradictions and uncertainties complicate prison management today almost as much as they did in 1870.

California's experience will be used as a source for suggesting generalizations about how scientific social movements serve as instruments of planned social change. Scientific social movements are becoming increasingly important instruments of planned change. Convictions and beliefs are not outdated in our modern era. The correctional movement—like psychoanalysis, conservation, and progressive education—aims at bringing about highly cherished

---

[1]American Correctional Association, *Manual of Correctional Standards*, revised edition. New York, American Correctional Association, 1960, 629 pp.

goals by combining faith in basic principles with periodic scientific evaluation of the means to check if means really serve the movement's specified ends.

Chapter 2

THE SCIENTIFIC SOCIAL MOVEMENT: A PATTERN OF PLANNED CHANGE

MOVEMENTS AS SOCIAL RESPONSES TO A PROBLEM

No society can survive without agreed upon laws and mores which enable people to react with each other on the basis of some degree of predictability. Prisons are among the agencies employed to control those who are not responsive to less drastic constraints. Most criminals are physically healthy and mentally alert. They usually are incarcerated against their will. Correction officials, be they humanitarian or punitively-oriented, therefore, have to be concerned with maintaining control over criminals to protect society.

The humanitarians believe that optimum protection is achieved when calculated risks are taken, to allow inmates some leeway to test their capacity for self-control while they are in prison and on parole. Maximum security measures are to be used only when inmates are unable to exercise any self-control, never as a means of punishment or retribution.

More custodially-oriented prison officials advocate a policy of tightness, in part because every extension of privileges has the inherent risk of abuse by those to whom it is extended. Escape from a minimum custody prison is easier than escape from a maximum custody prison. Science provides few guidelines to the questions of penal policy-making. Today, as well as ninety years ago, the field of correction is over-crowded with uncertainty. We still have few answers to the questions posed by Signor Scalia, the Inspector of Italy's prisons, at the first National Prison Congress in 1870:

> For the last 50 years, the efficiency of the different penitentiary systems has been carefully debated, but that question has

not yet made much progress; and, at present, as was the case a long time ago, the champions of different schools are ranged in the field of abstractions, to go over the same arguments, and to allege on both sides the same facts and experiments. Though chains have been broken, corporeal punishment has been abolished, though the prisoner receives a better treatment than heretofore, though indulgence and leniency have now superseded the severity of punishment, nobody can tell me whether and how far this humanitarian spirit has stopped the corrupting current of guilt; what have been the effects of such or such other punishment; and none can inform me why they have deemed it better to be more lenient or more severe; and the problem about relapse still remains unsolved.[1]

Penal reform ideas have been accepted because they appealed to humanitarian sentiments, not because there has been conclusive evidence that they will solve penal problems. Indeterminate sentences, parole, prison education, and treatment had a plausible rationale, but the participants of the Cincinnati Prison Congress espoused them without information about their impact on the reform of inmates. The fervor with which reformers worked for them was related to their philosophical orientation.

DIVERGENCE AND CONVERGENCE IN POLICY-MAKING

The general public is unaware of the existence of the Correctional Movement and its program. Popular expectations from prison management reflect a variety of partly contradictory philosophical objectives.

1. *Humanitarianism.* The idea of humane handling of all persons irrespective of the crime they may have committed. They are to be dealt with on the basis of our constitutional guarantees against "cruel and unusual punishment." Provision of decent food, shelter, medical care and recreational facilities are justified on that basis.
2. *Reform.* The idea of changing the personality and/or social adjustment potential of inmates, to increase the

[1]Signor Martino Beltrani Scalia: "Historical Sketch of National and International Penitentiary Conferences in Europe and America."

probability of their living within socially acceptable norms after release from prison.

3. *Control.* The idea of maintaining order in the prison, the the prevention of riots, and the protection from harm of prison personnel, property, and inmates.

4. *Punishment.* The idea of imprisonment as retribution, to cause the offender discomfort and suffering. It is often justified on the theory that punishment has deterrent effects on the offender himself and on potential offenders tempted to commit similar crimes.

Only the rare prison official approaches crime control from any one of these points of view. The attitudes co-exist in the thought processes of many citizens. There is widespread approval of the kind of mixed policy advocated by Chief Justice Earl Warren, who, as Governor of California, presided over that State's extensive reform of the correctional system:

> The idea of punishment has not and cannot entirely be abandoned. It should, however, be regarded as only one of the many possible devices for discipline, treatment and ultimately rehabilitation.[1]

Prison officials differ in the degree to which they emphasize one or the other idea. Those strongly inclined toward humanitarian reform procedures are usually just as concerned about their legal responsibilities to protect the public by keeping inmates under control as are those who put most stress on punishment and control functions of prisons. The latter also avow interest in rehabilitation. The two approaches differ in emphasis rather than in absolutes. They vary more in the means they advocate, than in the ends. There is considerable agreement about such criteria of correctional effectiveness as:

1. Avoidance of prison riots.
2. Adherence to prison rules.
3. Security of all prisoners and property.
4. Due process of law in prison management.
5. Avoidance of recidivism by discharged prisoners.

---

[1]Norman Fenton: *Group Counseling: A Preface to Its Use in Correctional and Welfare Agencies.* Sacramento, California, The County Project in Correctional Methods, Institute for the Study of Crime and Delinquency, 1961.

Controversies among prison officials about policy rarely involve these criteria, but the means most likely to advance their attainment. Officials who lean heavily towards humanitarian and reform-oriented ideas give more emphasis to the use of educational and treatment procedures than those who give a high priority to the punishment-control philosophy. Day-to-day prison management usually is a compromise between two polar orientations:

Reform Ideology

Education of inmates

Strengthening prisoner self-control

Social pressure on prisoners to live up to social expectations

Punishment Ideology

Degree of retribution related to offense

Police surveillance

Tough law enforcement

PUNISHMENT, EDUCATION, AND TREATMENT SCHOOLS OF THOUGHT

This model of policy alternatives is logical, but no substitute for empirical study of what prison officials actually think. It is what they think rather than what policies are publicly circulated that affect their day-to-day interaction with inmates. The identification with various penal points of view of employees of the California Department of Correction was, therefore, studied by means of an extensive attitude survey. The questionnaire, which was administered to large groups of employees at work, explored their personal identification with alternate administrative policies.[1] Sufficiently complete questionnaires, to be available for analysis, were returned by 94 per cent of the employees in 1959. A wide range of opinions was found in all categories of employees. But there were

---

[1]See Appendix B for a schedule of this attitude survey.

sufficiently clear cut differences in attitude patterns to infer the existence of three approximate schools of thought.

One of the key questions used to identify policy preferences of employees was a question asking them to rank the first three of eight alternate prison activities which in their view was making "the greatest impact on an offender's chances of reforming." Forty per cent made a relatively *punitive* response, selecting either "the experience of being behind bars," or "loss of freedom and civil rights." An *educational* emphasis was evident in the first choices of 31 per cent, who selected vocational education, academic education, industrial or agricultural programs. Only 23 per cent selected *therapeutic* alternatives, psychotherapy or group counseling as their first choice.[1] Punishment, education and treatment co-existed as favored approaches to the remaking of incarcerated men, in this order of emphasis.

Second choices of the employees showed a moderate degree of consistency with their first choice. As Chart 1 shows, more than one-half of the prison officials who made a punitive first choice made a punitive second choice. Conversely, almost 40 per cent of those whose first choice was psychotherapy, selected group counseling as their second choice. Very few chose one of the more punitive responses as the second activity likely to make "the greatest impact on an offender's chances of reforming."

The educationally-minded employees were not just "middle of the road" ideologists. They were more likely to select an educational activity as their second choice than either a punitive or a therapeutic one. But they leaned more towards treatment than punishment. Of the educators who did not choose an educational technique as the technique with the second greatest reform impact, the ratio of therapeutic to punitive choices was nearly 4:1.

The men who manage prisons in California and are responsible for planning the life activities of inmates were not of one mind. While nearly all would pay lip service to the objective that prisons should remake inmates, they differed in what means they regard as the most promising to achieve this objective.

Predominance of a punitive, educational, or therapeutic attitude cannot be inferred simply from a person's job category. Half

---

[1]See Table 5, page_____.

COMPARISON OF FIRST WITH SECOND CHOICES FROM AMONG EIGHT ALTERNATIVE ACTIVITIES RATED AS MAKING "THE GREATEST IMPACT ON AN OFFENDER'S CHANCES OF REFORMING"

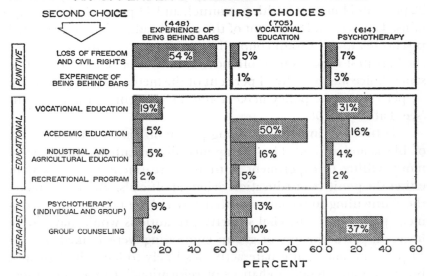

CHART 1

Based on responses to the following question: "Many activities in a prison are undertaken to help the inmates. Please select the three which, in your opinion, tend to make the greatest impact on an offender's chances of reforming. Write No. 1 next to your first choice, No. 2 next to your second choice, and No. 3 next to your third choice. Please rank only three."

> The experience of "being behind bars."
> Loss of freedom and civil rights.
> Recreational program.
> Group counseling program.
> Vocational education.
> Academic education.
> Industrial and agricultural education.
> Psychotherapy (individual and group).

A number of reform oriented activities were excluded from this multiple choice question, to keep it simple. For instance, the work of librarians was not given as one of the choices. Nor were such activities as radio, television, or movies singled out. It is possible that some of the respondents had these in mind when they considered choosing recreation as one of the three alternate activities.

of the custody administrators (correctional captains, lieutenants, and sergeants) thought that imprisonment and loss of civil rights had more impact on an offender's chances or reforming than academic or vocational training, psychotherapy, or group counseling. But this attitude was also shared by 30 per cent of the policy makers, 22 per cent of mental health personnel, and 44 per cent of the chaplains. Conversely, 18 per cent of the custody administrators selected psychotherapy or group counseling as the activity likely to make the "greatest impact on an offender's chances of reforming." The same choice was made by 64 per cent of the mental health personnel, 52 per cent of the policy makers and 44 per cent of the chaplains (see Table 3, p. 56).

Differences in outlook among prison officials are not a matter of black and white. The therapeutically oriented officials were more willing to experiment with new treatment programs than either the punitive or education oriented officials. But even among those unwilling to recommend that any risk be taken with a treatment program, if custodial security precautions would have to be lowered, psychotherapy or group counseling were ranked first by 14 per cent among alternate activities likely to have the "greatest impact on an offender's chances of reforming." Conversely, those willing to take risks with custodial security in order to introduce a new treatment program included 36 per cent whose first choice was punitive. They selected loss of freedom and civil rights or "the experience of being behind bars" as the activity that tends to make the greatest impact on an offender's chance of reforming (see Table 1).

Divergencies in attitudes between custody and treatment people are sufficiently patterned to provide a focus of power struggles in prisons and ideological conflicts among categories of employees. They have been well-documented in a growing body of empirical study of prisons as a social system.[1] But the existence of convergence of attitudes among employees with different jobs and polarized the-

---

[1]This area of sociological investigation was recently reviewed by the Conference Group on Correctional Organization, sponsored by the Social Science Research Council. Richard A. Cloward, Donald R. Cressey, George H. Grosses, Richard McCleery, Lloyd E. Ohlin, Gresham M. Sykes, and Sheldon L. Messinger, *Theoretical Studies in Social Organization of the Prison.* New York, Research Council, 1960.

oretical differences has sometimes been overlooked by analysts of prison. This convergence is facilitated by the educators. Their representatives have been employed in prisons for a longer time than have the therapists. They are reform oriented and, like the treatment specialists, tend to be better educated than the custody

TABLE 1

ACTIVITY CHOSEN AS MAKING THE "GREATEST IMPACT ON AN OFFENDER'S CHANCE OF REFORMING" FROM AMONG EIGHT ALTERNATIVES BY ATTITUDES FAVORABLE TO RISK TAKING WITH NEW TREATMENT PROGRAMS

| Activity Chosen to Have Greatest Impact* | *Willingness to Recommend Risk Taking**￼* | | |
	None (N = 1498) (41%)	Some (N = 1559) (43%)	A Great Deal (N = 552) (15%)
Punitive			
Loss of freedom and civil rights	31	26	25
Experience of "being behind bars"	15	11	11
Educational			
Vocational Education	20	19	19
Academic Education	10	9	9
Industrial and Agricultural	3	3	3
Recreational Program	2	1	1
Therapeutic			
Psychotherapy (individual and group)	8	23	24
Group Counseling	6	5	6
No responses	5	3	2
Totals	100	100	100

*The same question used in Chart 1.

**The employees of the Department of Correction were divided into three categories, "None," "Some," and "A great deal" on the basis of their responses to the following question: "Which of the following policies would you favor with regard to experimentation with new treatment programs if you were a member of a staff advisory committee on institutional policy?" Check *only* one:

1. No treatment program should be instituted if custodial security precautions would have to be lowered.
2. Treatment programs can be instituted even though a moderate increase in the probability of escape is involved.
3. Custodial considerations are secondary in setting up a treatment program (except for the care of dangerous offenders), since the most important principle in organizing a prison program is the need of defenders.

employees. They are as skeptical about the impact of punitive techniques as were the more vociferous treatment enthusiasts. But they also were not sold on therapy. Two-thirds of the employees whose "greatest impact" choice had been vocational education, chose academic, industrial, or agricultural education as the second most important program to affect an offender's chances of reforming (see Chart 1, p. 29).

THE COMMON IDEOLOGICAL CORE

Care must be taken not to exaggerate contrast between these schools of thought. All tend to accept the principle of some punishment for men convicted of a crime. All avow a belief in the moral necessity of reform of inmates. For instance, reformers have justified the building of a swimming pool as a privilege available to inmates whose adjustment to prison life warrants it. Some more punitively oriented employees regard this as being "too soft." But even in the minimum custody section of the California Institute for Men at Chino, where an inmate can swim in a pool once a week, he is severely punished.

He is in prison. He has lost much social status, a loss not readily recouped even after his release. The stigma of "ex-convict" remains with him for life. The prisoner also loses his civil rights. He has little privacy. He can make few decisions for himself. He cannot have heterosexual relationships, nor be with his family. Choices of what he eats are severely restricted. He is required to live close to a subsistence level, without many of the comforts that even poor people in the United States can often enjoy. He is forced to associate with other criminals, some of whom are unstable and even dangerous.

Educators and treatment people, those who favor the reform point of view, think that these consequences of imprisonment are punishment enough. They see no need to aggravate the prisoner's punishment by the enforcement of harsh rules not required for safety reasons. They value educational and treatment programs as most likely to contribute to the rehabilitation of inmates.

Those with a more punitive orientation are not usually opposed to education and treatment. They assign a higher priority to punishment aspects and stress their treatment potential. Prison psychiatrists and social workers, no matter how dedicated to their conviction about the importance of treatment, rarely were without sentiments favoring some of the many punitive aspects of prison life. Only the pathological sadist would be without compassion for prisoners whom he sees under conditions of unhappiness or intense suffering.

This overlapping of attitudes and objectives provides a basis of accommodation and compromise of different categories of officials within the correctional movement. From its inception in 1870, reformers, including the educators and therapists, have worked with more custody-oriented officials who pay lip service to the goals of the reformers as spelled out in the *Declaration of Principles*. Reformers, in turn, have usually been moderate in pushing new ideas too far too quickly.

THE PROBLEM OF UNCERTAINTY

Agreement about the objectives of correctional effectiveness (ends) does not resolve differences in priority of techniques (means) that exist between those who are more treatment or more punishment-oriented, particularly since there is public support for all of these ideologies. "Throw the book" at convicts is as popular a slogan as "Give them a chance." Prison administrators rarely have an explicit mandate on just how much treatment and how much control should be built into the day-to-day operation of a particular institution. They must make choices among several policy alternatives.

Risk-taking is a function not only of prison administrators but of all professionals. Prison administrators must make decisions about how to deal with criminals, who are feared, despised, and hated by the public, with only clinical experience of *uncertain* relevancy to guide them. They deal with a chronically recidivist population. Fewer than 12 per cent of the males in California prisons had no prior "experience" in juvenile detention homes, jails, or prisons. One out of twenty had four or more *prior* prison commitments. There were 803 men or 4 per cent of all male prisoners, under life sentence.[1] Are these men beyond hope of reform? Which sex criminals must be kept under maximum security conditions? When is a murderer ready to be sent to a minimum custody forestry camp, from which he could easily escape? When can he be paroled? Every decision requires the making of an educated guess. Penal administrators and parole board members must answer these questions. If an error is made, and a parolee commits a new crime, the deed cannot be undone. If no paroles were made, 95 per cent of all inmates would still be entitled to be released at the expiration of their sentence. Many new prisons would have to be built. Other than their personal experience, parole board members have only statistical information about past experiences of categories of inmates to guide them. Prediction of the future behavior of any particular inmate whose term of imprisonment has to be set involves elements of uncertainty.

When custody is an over-riding requirement, as it is with dangerous and mentally disturbed prisoners, maximum controls are maintained. Such inmates are carefully guarded. They are rarely allowed to meet their visitors except through a glass partition. They have few opportunities to test their capacity for self-control. But with most prisoners, administrators must take chances of abuse of privileges as part of the price of extending them. In minimum custody prisons, trustee posts, and pre-release living units, prisoners may be able to escape without much difficulty. They can abuse their freedoms in other ways as well. But treatment-oriented persons strongly stand for such a substitution as "brains for bars."[2] They argue that it is better to give inmates a chance to demonstrate their capacity to live up to social expectations while still under legal surveillance, than to wait until the completion of their sentence and their unconditional release. Chance-taking is one of the chief functions of management.

Correctional administrators function somewhat like doctors with cancer patients. They must act decisively in a field of great

---

[1]Department of Corrections, State of California, *Characteristics of Felon Population of California State Prisons by Institutions as of December 31, 1961.* Sacramento, California, Department of Corrections, Research Division, Administrative Statistics Section, mimeographed release, dated February 28, 1962.

[2]James V. Bennett: "Building for Corrections," *Architectural Record,* Vol. 126, December, 1959:216.

uncertainty but of considerable importance to the public. There is evidence that some patients can be "cured" symptomatically, even though the cause of the tissue damage is unknown. In others, the spread of the malignancy can be controlled, but no one knows for how long. And there are those who are hopelessly ill, hopeless at the present stage of knowledge. So with prisoners, the administrators may "cure" without knowing why; they may control anti-social behavior for an unpredictable length of time; or they may fail with hopeless cases.

Little is known about the differential control potential of punitive, educational, and treatment-oriented programs. Major violations occur under all systems. Helen Witmer and Edith Tufts, in a thoughtful survey of evaluative research in delinquency in 1954, concluded with the following sobering observation, "What does all this add up to in knowledge about how to prevent or reduce delinquency? The answer, unfortunately, is: 'With certainty, rather little.' "[1]

Even without certainty on the outcome of educational and treatment programs, the humanitarians espouse them. In the absence of negative findings, they can nourish a hope that their approach has the optimum potential for achieving some degree of control. They also *believe* in the *moral* superiority of their policies.

NEWISM

Scientific knowledge often falls short of being conclusive. Such questions as "Shall the patient breast or bottle feed her baby?" or "Shall drug addicts be imprisoned or hospitalized?" have to be resolved without the sense of security that could be derived from well-documented evidence on the consequences of each practice for particular types of persons. Pediatricians, social workers, and judges must make choices about what to recommend on the basis of scientific evidence *plus* tradition, agency policies, and hunches from personal experience. Rarely can social practitioners know enough to warrant making recommendations with a high degree of confidence.

Individual practitioners differ greatly in their methods of

---

[1]Helen L. Witmer and Edith Tufts: *The Effectiveness of Delinquency Prevention Programs.* Washington, D. C., U. S. Children's Bureau, 1954.

dealing with the *uncertainty aspect* of their work. Some attempt to ignore or deny it. Others try to differentiate between what they know, what others may know, and perhaps what no one really knows. And all practitioners must rely to some extent on reassurance derived from speculative ideas which are socially (rather than scientifically) validated by being accepted by a social movement.

In tradition-bound societies the old-fashioned is presumed to have validity. Herbalists make claims for the curative powers of their wares by the appeal, "They worked for our forefathers; so why shouldn't they work for us?" The opposite philosophy is common in modern societies. We shall designate it as *newism*: the presumption that new developments or practices are superior to those not quite so new, or old. When such practices become a program advocated by a self-conscious group, a social movement is born.

Newism is an ideology which encourages change. Tradition or the *status quo* is evaluated negatively. The attribute of novelty is presumed to indicate validity. Newism is appealed to in merchandising that aims to produce psychic obsolescence for last year's model car. Plausible rather than well-documented facts are used to support the theory that stylistic changes also represent a gain in operating efficiency and durabililty. Newism helps to explain why educators are often ready to embrace "new curriculum" ideas without research analysis of the old. New techniques of treatment, even before they can be thoroughly tested, tend to take the place of older techniques, whose limitations have become known by experience. *Life* magazine notes that many doctors are persuaded—and many patients want—"new drugs simply because they are new, not because they are necessarily better than something old or cheap."[1] Newism validates fads and fashions by appeal to the criterion of "common sense," in which the mores rather than the scientific methods provide the sanction for a belief in what is effective.

Newistic movements flourish in countries with rapid rates of

[1]"Big Pill to Swallow: The Wonder Drug Makers Get Handsome Profits from Their Captive Consumers," *Life*, Vol. 48, February 15, 1960:98. For technical details see Mindel C. Sheps, "The Clinical Value of Drugs: Sources of Evidence," read before the Medical Care Section, American Public Health Association, October 31, 1960. Also John Lear, Science Editor, "Do We Need a Census of Worthless Drugs?" *Saturday Review of Literature*, Vol. 42, May 7, 1960:53.

change. They serve a number of social functions. They confer status on the people associated with the innovation and provide an opportunity for new experience. They also serve the advancement of knowledge. The predisposition to accept the attribute of newness as an index to progress makes it possible for innovations to survive through a developmental period, long enough to be perfected technically and to be tested by scientific methods.

Newism is commonplace in the helping professions, where alternate treatment procedures are in vogue. For instance, psychoanalysis is practiced by psychiatrists, psychologists, and social workers claiming adherence to several schools of thought.[1] Group workers, recreation specialists and adult educators offer overlapping programs of work with groups. The claims made for each treatment procedure, like all ideas, compete in the market place of man's mind. In the very long-run their acceptance is affected by their scientific validity. But at the stage when scientific evidence is not yet conclusive, practitioners derive much confidence from identification with a social group that espouses one set of ideas, while others are ignored or less valued.[2] They derive reassurances —often false reassurance from the identification of newness with goodness or progress. But this is what often happens in the scientific professions. The history of applied science is the story not only of what men were able to prove scientifically, but also of societal dynamics.

Reliance on newistic validation by substituting reference group supports for evidence, is not usually uniform for all aspects of the same treatment program. Social (as against scientific) sanction is least relied upon when there is supportive evidence that a technique works as in the selection of prison inmates for vocational and academic training. Aptitude tests useful in the making of

---

[1]Ruth L. Monroe: *Schools of Psychoanalytic Thought.* New York, The Dryden Press, 1955; Patric Mullahy, *Oedipus Myth and Complex.* New York, Hermitage Press, 1948.

[2]For a good study illustrating this generalization, see Herbert Menzel and Elihu Katz, "Social Relations and Innovation in the Medical Profession: The Epidemiology of a New Drug," *Public Opinion Quarterly,* Vol. XIX, No. 4, Winter, 1955-56:337-352. Opinion leaders were found to play a major role in the adoption of a new drug. The timing of its adoption by individuals was related to the role of each doctor in the medical community of his town.

placement decisions have been developed. Newism tends to become important to sanction actions where there is no evidence or in situations which are objectively only vaguely understood. It is relied upon heavily to decide how prisoners should be treated—through academic education, vocational education, psychotherapy, social casework, or group counseling. It is equally relied on when the decision is on what kind of specialists should give treatment, or what kind of training will best prepare him for the job. There are few empirical guidelines to answer these questions. A non-scientific, but socially sanctioned enthusiasm is accepted as a substitute rationale for decision making.

THE PATTERNING OF SCIENTIFIC REFORM MOVEMENTS

The capacity to form and maintain social movements is one of the characteristics that distinguishes *homo sapiens* from other social animal species—the ants, the bees, and the buffaloes. Reform movements, unlike revolutions, aim to bring about change within the existing order of things, they accept most of the underlying values of the present social system.

Confidence in a solution played an important role in every *religious* and *political* reform movement. It has been a factor, for example, in Protestantism, in Women's Suffrage, or in the Townsend Movement. Historians and social scientists who studied these in accordance with a well-defined program have shown them to be greatly affected by such factors as the personality of the leader, ideological concepts, social and power forces.[1]

Reliance on these cultural elements is less characteristic of a scientific reform movement, like psychoanalysis, conservation, public health, and progressive education. Ideas presently accepted by these movements are thought to be more than just normatively "right." They are also regarded as being scientifically valid. Dogma is most likely to flourish in areas of action for which science presently provides few clues for decision-making. Such principles may

---

[1]See, for instance, Joyce O. Hertzler: *Society in Action.* New York, Dryden Press, 1954; Hadley Cantril: *The Psychology of Social Movements.* New York, John Wiley and Sons, 1941; and C. Wendell King: *Social Movements in the United States.* New York, Random House, 1956.

be pronounced with passion to be taken for granted rather than tested. But the idea of their being subject to verification is not denied.

Each of these movements involves a restricted group of specialists. Leaders attain and retain their influence on the basis of reputation built in great part on technical qualifications and scientific achievements. Advancements in knowledge make it likely that the latest technique is soon to be replaced by an improvement. Ideas advanced by a scientific social movement, therefore, tend to have a limited life expectancy. No dogma is thought to be beyond the realm of being tested empirically.

No two reform movements are alike. They differ in objectives, the circumstances that give rise to them, the methods employed, and the personality of those who lead them. Social science studies of their pattern of development shows, however, the presence of analogous characteristics. Joyce O. Hertzler employs an imaginative analytic model of several overlapping stages to describe them. It will be used in this study, with several modifications. The description of a social movement in terms of successive, though overlapping stages of development introduces a more rigid structure on historical events than is warranted. It is more accurate to view social movements as a series of events that differ in the function they serve the total social system. There are events that make up crisis conditions which precede every reform. They are followed by incubation processes, initiation events, institutionalization procedures, formalism and decay indications, and reorganization.

1. *The Crisis*

Events that are indicative of a sense of urgency for change. There is widespread dissatisfaction with the status quo. Individuals are unable to find a solution within presently sanctioned means. In a scientific reform movement, the crisis always involves complex uncertainties about the state of knowledge. It is viewed as grossly insufficient for rational decision making.

Widespread recognition of the existence of a crisis mobilizes public support favorable to change. It also discourages vested interests, who have supported the old order, by placing them on the defensive.

2. Incubation

Exploration by a leader or group of leaders of carefully planned alterations of existing institutional arrangements. In a religious or political reform movement there tends to be stress on the charismatic, or inspired personality of the leader.[1] In a scientific reform movement there tends to be more emphasis on the technical competence of persons in leadership positions.

3. Initiation

Ethusiastic innovation of a planned program aiming to attain more effectively accepted institutional values than has been possible under previously tried arrangements. The reforms—actions that are regarded as being new—will be viewed as if they were valid. In a scientific reform movement, innovations are viewed more tentatively, they are more likely to be termed "experimental." While anything new implies that there is a possibility of making a significant discovery, there also is intellectual acceptance of the prospect that the innovated program may fail to accomplish its purposes. This intellectual awareness of the possibility of failure is not tantamount to its emotional acceptance. In every scientific social movement, the innovations which are proposed are characterized by a hope that they work. There is an optimistic fervor.

4. Institutionalization

The development of organizational routines and the adaptation of previously existing institutional arrangements to implement the new program. The innovations become stabilized. Executive direction is delegated by the pioneering leaders to more organization-minded men. In a scientific reform movement, there tends to be more stress on the scientific respectability of the new program than on symbolic attributes like novelty, popularity, or "folksiness." Research is undertaken to displace newness with evidence of validity as the basis for continued acceptance of the idea.

---

[1] A concept made popular by Max Weber to designate a quality of superior and inspired wisdom which followers project upon their leaders. H. H. Gerth and C. Wright Mills: *From Max Weber: Essays in Sociology.* London, Kegan, Paul, Trench, Trubner and Company, 1947. Also see Roberto Michels, *First Lectures in Political Sociology*, translated, with an introduction by Alfred de Grazia. Minneapolis, Minnesota, University of Minnesota Press, 1949.

5. *Formalism and Decay*

Reform ideas tend to persist in spite of increasing evidence that they fall short of meeting their stated objectives. Routinization occurs when there is more stress on the stabilization of the means, "the program," than on attainment of the objectives for which they had been introduced. Suggestions for improvement are resisted even when there is evidence that an innovation might serve the reform program better in meeting its goals.

Formalism and decay are minimized in scientific reform movements because there is a commitment to weigh issues, at least in part, on the basis of scientific knowledge. The scientific credo that all knowledge is only approximate serves as an antidote to the entrenchment of formalism in a scientific reform movement.

While political and religious panacea are believed to be inherently valid, no scientific program is theoretically beyond being tested by research, even when those who employ it believe in its effectiveness with fervor.

6. *Reorganization*

The shortcomings of the status quo become recognized. Steps are taken to initiate alterations. A reformation of the reform is undertaken. Earlier innovations, accepted in part because of their newistic appeal, are displaced by still newer and equally plausible proposals. A number of splinter groups may emerge, each claiming to be the true inheritor of the goals that inspired the original reform. A new social movement is born. In a scientific reform movement, the emphasis of new schools of thought tends to be that they correct previous errors and incorporate all of the most recently discovered knowledge.

THE CENTRAL HYPOTHESIS

Correctional reform in America, if not the entire world, is the ideology of a scientific reform movement. Its history in California can be looked at as a sequence of events with the aforementioned functions. New treatment ideas were successively favored. In the nineteenth century, the abolition of neglect and torture were the primary preoccupations. During the twentieth century, there was increasing emphasis on classification and differential treatment of the various categories of inmates, providing them with work opportunities and education. Since 1954, the favored program has been therapeutic, particularly group treatment. It grew by virtue of deliberate administrative encouragement.

In a highly structured organization like the California Department of Corrections, this last fact alone might have been sufficient to co-opt civil servants to favor the new program. But evidence will be presented that the idea was rooted in more substance than mere official encouragement from the top down. It was re-enforced by enthusiasm in the ranks. A significant minority of the employees embraced the idea with a greater personal investment than would be true of routine administrative instructions. As a result top echelon correctional administrators could place increasing reliance on the form of prisoner-correctional employee interaction. Had there been much opposition, the program would have proceeded more cautiously, if at all.[1] Milton Burdman, Chief of Classification and Treatment, wrote in 1957:

> It is my strong belief that group counseling as now operated gives us a most important avenue to provide constructive experiences for prison inmates and their relationship with staff and with each other. The personnel participating in this program are doing a difficult and challenging job and in this are charting a new course for the correctional field.[2]

He was seconded by many, such as Lawrence M. Stutsman, then an Associate Superintendent, who called group counseling the "major new happening in the field of corrections during the last few decades."[3]

A Federal prison official, who had no personal experience with the program, stated that:

> California's program of group counseling, if we understand its objectives, commands serious attention. . . . It seeks to

---

[1]The Department did not insist that the Vacaville Medical Facility introduce group counseling, although its Deputy Director of Classification and Treatment had demonstrated the procedure at Vacaville in the hope that it would be adapted there.

[2]Milton Burdman: "This Very Vital Departmental Program," *Group Counseling Newsletter,* Vol. 1, October, 1957.

[3]Lawrence M. Stutsman: "What About Group Counseling?" *Group Counseling Newsletter,* Vol. 1, October, 1957.

broaden the base of institutional treatment services by involving increasing numbers of institutional personnel within the framework of the treatment program. It is a device through which, hopefully, offenders may gain greater insight into their problems and find a basis for the modification of their attitudes. It is an effort to resolve traditional conflicts between personnel and inmates and provide a background for closer mutual understanding, confidence and cooperation. These objectives, if reached only in part, will more than serve to justify the work which has gone into the program.[1]

Group treatment was advocated as something more than a technique. It also embodied the hopes of many as a progressive step in the correctional field.

If this social movement hypothesis is applicable to the California correctional reform history, it will be possible to examine its contemporary and future development as something other than a sequence of accidental events. They become part of the predictable pattern, within which men can strive to accomplish their objectives by planning.

---

[1] H. G. Moller: "Notes on a Progress Report on Group Counseling in the California Prisons," *Proceedings of the 86th Annual Congress of Correction.* New York, American Correctional Association, 1956.

Chapter 3

THE CALIFORNIA SETTING

When the first American Congress of Corrections met in 1870, California was still a frontier state. Its public services were rough hewn, but it had a sophisticated representative in the Reverend James Woodworth, Secretary of the State Prison Commission. He was a humanitarian, with ideas far different from the reality of prison conditions then existing. Many of the county jails and the state prison at San Quentin were a living hell, lorded over by political appointees. Perhaps this is why he was moved to read a paper at the Cincinnati Congress, advocating professional standards for prison officials, and the participation of women in penal administration. He said in part:

> The task of changing bad men and women into good ones is not one to be confided to the first comers. It is a serious charge, demanding thorough preparation, entire self-devotion, a calm and cautious judgment, great firmness of purpose and steadiness of action, large experience, a true sympathy and morality above suspicion. Prison officers, therefore, need a special education for their work; special training schools should be instituted for them, and prison administration should be raised to the dignity of a profession.[1]

More than seventy years were to pass before his sentiments were to find expression in state policy.

---

[1]James Woodworth in Prison Association of New York, *Twenty-sixth Annual Report of the Executive Committee of the Prison Association of New York and Accompanying Documents for the Year 1870, to Which Is Appended the Papers and Proceedings of the National Congress on Penitentiary and Reformatory Discipline Held in Cincinnati, Ohio, October 12 to 18, 1870.* New York, The Angus Company, 1871.

THE OLD ORDER

Prison conditions were periodically scandalous in California until World War II. In 1938, Clinton R. Duffy, the son of a prison guard at San Quentin, was appointed warden. Duffy reports that he had to put an end to many practices inconsistent with humanitarian ideals:

> This was a supposedly enlightened age, but up in the cell blocks—in the row called "Siberia"—men were being forced to stand on a 9 inch circle for hours at a time. If they moved or talked or turned around, they were dragged into a back room and beaten with a hose or leather straps. Prison officials were depriving inmates of decent clothing, blankets and other simple necessities so that they could claim savings for the taxpayers, and the food was often sour and half cooked.
>
> The dungeon was being used more and more instead of being closed. It was a black tunnel about 50 feet long with seven small cells on each side. The ancient mass of rock and concrete had the musty odor of a tomb. No sunlight had touched its moldy walls for almost 90 years, and the foul air had no place to go, for there were no windows and the cell doors were hand-forged iron. Each cell was nothing more than a niche cut into the stone, and the walls and floors were bare. There was no light, no bed, no ventilation, no toilet facilities, not even a bench. There were sometimes three or four men in one cell. Prisoners slept on the damp floor with one blanket, if they were lucky, and they got bread and water at the whims of the guards. Not all of these men were vicious criminals. Some were shoved into the hole because they had turned in a bad piece of jute cloth, or quarrelled with their con boss, or wise-cracked to a guard.[1]

In 1938, California had two large state prisons. Little was done there to rehabilitate the inmates; much was done to embitter them against society. Each warden was a political appointee. He had little security, but while in office he had the powers of a feudal baron. Guards and other staff members were poorly paid, subject to political influence, and often ill qualified to perform their difficult tasks. Few statewide standards were or could be enforced at the cell block level.

---

[1]Clinton T. Duffy: *San Quentin: The Story of a Prison*. London, Peter Davies, 1951.

THE NEW ORDER

Conditions changed drastically between 1944 and 1961. California's State Prisons' population more than quadrupled from 5,710 in 1944 to over 23,000 in 1961. The Department of Corrections also acquired jurisdiction over more than 8,000 men and women on parole. A network of parole offices reached into every California community.

The gas chamber at San Quentin probably was still the most notoriously publicized Departmental facility, although it was used for an average of no more than seven to eight executions a year after 1955, less than one per 1,000 of those sent to prison. For all others, control and care were being planned for the possible day of release back into society, with hope that they would not become recidivists. Not only secure custody, but also education and treatment became central functions of imprisonment.

The casual passerby of one of California's nine major institutions and twenty-seven permanent camps would not notice this new spirit. He cannot look much beyond the barbed wire fences to find out why the Department of Corrections was renowned for being technically well-managed, humanitarian, experimental, and research-oriented.

Before World War II, men with education and humanitarian ideals had little to attract them to state prison work. But by 1959, most of the prison system's policy makers were at least college graduates (85%); 45 per cent had Master's or doctoral degrees. Even among the correctional officers, as guards had been renamed, 32 per cent had some college education.

The state prison system in 1960 measured up well in terms of four out of five of the operational criteria for correctional effectiveness which were previously listed:

1. No major prison riots had occurred since the Department was established. Minor disturbances were quickly brought under control.
2. Prison rule violations were no major managerial problem.
3. Prisoners and property were generally secure from attack. Pilfering offenses of inmates against each other or against free personnel were uncommon, although they do occur from time to time.

4. Prison management followed due process of law procedures. There was no cruel or unusual punishment. Humanitarian principles governed interaction between staff and inmates. No major disciplinary action was taken without a formal hearing at which the inmate was free to tell his side of the story.

5. But there was still considerable recidivism among those discharged from prisons.[1] Imprisonment for a large proportion of the inmates is still a revolving door; discharge is likely to be an interlude until they will be re-apprehended for violation of parole or on a new offense.

Law and order in a prison are not enough. The probability is more than 95 per cent that a California State prison inmate will be released. Unless something is done to change the conditions under which criminals first became deviants, many can be expected to continue in criminal careers. This fact, along with the humanitarian outlook of many prison administrators, led to an emphasis on reform treatment through a variety of programs including vocational training, religious counseling, academic education, and psycho-social therapies. The rationale of each of these treatment programs was that a prescribed social experience tends to influence inmates or parolees to live their lives in a socially acceptable manner after they leave prison. For instance:

Religious Counseling — Touch a man's soul and convert him. He will be better able to control his evil impulses.

Vocational Education — Teach a man a skill to *earn* a good living. He will not need to commit crimes to get money for the things he needs to sustain himself.

Academic Education — Educate a man so that he will acquire varied interests that can be a basis for meaningful associations

---

[1]Statistics on recidivism are not kept current. This is a complex research undertaking. It is not yet known how many of the offenders who participate in the various current treatment programs will be recidivists. Of the male felons in prison on December 31, 1961, only 11.9 per cent had no prior commitment, and 41.4 per cent had been in jail or had a juvenile commitment. The others had been in a prison or jail at least once. (From Department of Corrections, State of California, Research Division, Administrative Statistics Section, *Characteristics of Felon Population of California State Prisons by Institution as of December 31, 1961*. Sacramento, California, Department of Corrections, February 28, 1962. Mimeographed report.)

with decent people. He will then be less tempted to associate
with riff-raff.

Reference Group — Change a man's anti-social reference group
identification to association with the patterns of socially-
acceptable groups.

Social Casework and Psychotherapy — Develop a man's insight
and ego-strength. He will be better able to control his anti-
social impulses.

There is no shortage of illustrations of how a particular criminal
reformed after exposure to a religious, educational, skill-training,
casework or group association experience. But there are even more
cases of return to a criminal career after exposure to such treatment.
These failures leave correctional administrators uncertain about
how to answer evaluative questions, such as:

1. Which reform experience or combination of experiences
   is the treatment of choice for specific cases?
2. Was the reform experience a causal factor in an inmate's
   ultimate change or lack of it?
3. Who are the untreatable cases, i.e., criminals incapable of
   being reformed by techniques currently known?

The Department has gone beyond asking these questions. In
1957, legislative authorization was obtained to establish a Research
Division. In 1962, it included a staff of about forty professionals
who were busy in a variety of evaluative research programs and
who encouraged basic correctional research by several university-
employed specialists.

THE GROUP TREATMENT PROGRAM

All correctional reform programs are equal in the fact that they
rest on plausible, but as yet not verified, assumptions regarding
their effectiveness. But in 1962 in California they were not given
equal organizational encouragement. Foremost administrative emphasis was placed on the expansion of group treatment, either group
psychotherapy or group counseling. Both can be conducted without lowering security requirements, in contrast to such reform programs as minimum custody prisons, early paroles, and probation.

Few additional staff persons have to be hired. One leader can interact with more inmates than when counseling inmates individually.

Group psychotherapy, as this term is officially used, denotes professional treatment. Leadership is by a social worker, psychologist, or psychiatrist, for whom this work is part of the job requirement. All of the leaders are expected to have had some formal training in guiding people in a therapeutically-oriented group experience. It is generally presumed that they use scientific techniques to involve inmates in a relatively deep form of psychological treatment. It varies in intensity and requires from one to two hours weekly. Personality change is believed to be a probable outcome.

Group counseling refers to treatment under the leadership of clinically untrained employees, such as correctional officers (guards), shop foremen, or administrators.[1] It is believed to be a less deep experience. It is founded on the belief that mere association of a troubled person with an accepting fellow-human being has a treatment potential. It uses the form of small group discussions for usually one and one-half hours a week to effect healthy human relationships between inmates and correctional employees during the remaining 160. Group counseling taps unused treatment potentials among those employees having the most association with inmates. It has been viewed more as an educational or recreational than a personality changing technique. But the objectives outlined for group counseling in 1957 had much in common with those of group psychotherapy:

1. To develop a group setting for the inmates to study their own and each other's feelings and attitudes under the helpful and accepting auspices of the group leader.
2. To assist inmates in recognizing that their own problems are not unique. Others have the same distortions of feelings. Inmates can profit from seeing how others strive to face and deal with simliar problems.
3. To help inmates to adjust to the frustrations, which are an

---

[1] Outside California quite different models of treatment are referred to as *group counseling.* Hanna Grunwald, Supervisor of Group Counseling at the Brooklyn Bureau of Social Service and Children's Aid Society, regards it as a form of casework with a group of persons with similar problems. Hanna Grunwald, "Group Counseling in Combatting Delinquency," *Federal Probation,* Vol. 22, December, 1958.

unalterable part of prison life, as a prelude to better adjustment after release to society. This may be done by patient
and calm discussions among the group of conditions of
institutional living and of the reasons for various rules and
regulations which are imposed by the prison authorities.
Inmates should be permitted to ventilate frustration by
telling about their grievances.

4. To help the inmates recognize the possible significance of
    emotional conflict as underlying their criminal acts.

5. To permit the inmate to learn about how his personality
    affects others.

6. To help the inmate understand the world of fantasy, and
    how costly a part it may play in his social adjustment. Any
    disturbed, unhappy individual may find relief in day-
    dreaming. The inmate's daydreaming is more costly to
    him because it may lead to criminal behavior and to prison.

7. To begin planning for parole adjustment by discussing its
    problems with other inmates and group leader.

8. To improve the emotional climate of the institution. This
    could contribute to the transformation of the prison into
    a therapeutic community.[1]

Group counseling is predominantly non-directive, but has a
more eclectic theoretical orientation than most forms of group
psychotherapy where rationale is largely based on psychology and
personality theory. Group counseling objectives reflect a combined
psychological, psychiatric, and sociological view of criminal behavior, including the hope that groups can develop into reference
groups for re-learning and re-socialization.[2]

---

[1]Paraphrased from Norman Fenton: *An Introduction to Group Counseling in
Correctional Service.* Sacramento, California, The Department of Corrections, 1957.
Over the years, greater stress was placed on group counseling as a part of a total
milieu to influence inmates. See Norman Fenton: *Group Counseling: A Preface to
Its Use in Correctional and Welfare Agencies.* Sacramento, California, the County
Project in Correctional Methods under the auspices of the Institute for the Study of
Crime and Delinquency, 1961.

[2]Marshall Clinard: "The Group Approach to Social Reintegration," *American Sociological Review,* Vol. 14, April, 1949; also Donald R. Cressey: "Changing
Criminals: The Application of the Theory of Differential Association," *The American Journal of Sociology,* Vol. 41:116-120, September, 1955. This sociological approach
is also an acknowledged part of the rationale of "Guided Group Interaction" at High-

Group treatment in prison began as "experiments" to counter-act the *prisonization tendency* of inmates to conform to a pattern of social, criminal, and anti-administration expectations of the inmate subculture.[1] Group treatment blossomed into a major institutional program to accomplish the administrative objective of influencing incarcerated men to guide their conduct by socially and organizationally acceptable mores. Among the employees, active as leaders in January, 1959, were eighty-eight who reported themselves as doing group psychotherapy and 654 others who were doing group counseling. In addition, there were 514 staff persons who once had been group leaders, but were not then performing this role. Thus at one time or another over one-third of the Department's employees served as group leaders (see Chart 2).

Group treatment was not the sole jurisdictional concern of any one profession. It was an activity that transcended traditional job categories and administrative distinction. Group leadership was proportionately most prevalent among employees whose regular work includes psycho-social treatment, the mental health personnel, parole officers, chaplains, and educators. But even among the custody administrators and policy makers, more than half were leading or had previously led a group. Slightly more than one-fourth of all correctional officers (27 per cent) were, or had been, group counselors. Even 5 per cent of the clerical and office staff had volunteered to take a counseling group.

Many strategic reasons help to explain the decision to encourage group treatment, even before its effectiveness for specific purposes could be supported by evidence. Group treatment is relatively economical, a great attraction to prison administrators chronically plagued by tight budgets and shortages of clinically trained person-

---

field, New Jersey. See Lloyd W. McCorkle, Albert Elias and F. Lovell Bixby: *The Highfield Story*. New York, Henry Holt and Company, 1958.

[1]The prisonization phenomenon was identified by Donald Clemmer in his already, classic study *The Prison Community*. New York, Rinehart and Company, 1958. (Reprint of the first edition, published in 1940.) Clemmer's description of the inmate social system has stimulated much subsequent research on prisons and their culture. The treatment programs of the California Department of Correction represent a calculated administrative effort to reduce the anti-social influences of inmate mores and codes of conduct on incarcerated persons and to replace them with administratively approved behavior patterns that serve re-socialization objectives.

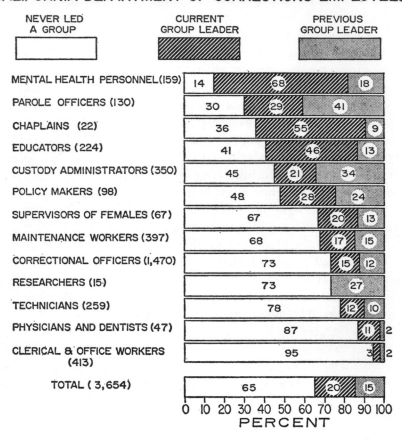

EXPERIENCE AS LEADER
IN GROUP TREATMENT PROGRAMS
CALIFORNIA DEPARTMENT OF CORRECTIONS EMPLOYEES

NEVER LED A GROUP   CURRENT GROUP LEADER   PREVIOUS GROUP LEADER

Category	Never Led	Current	Previous
MENTAL HEALTH PERSONNEL (159)	14	68	18
PAROLE OFFICERS (130)	30	29	41
CHAPLAINS (22)	36	55	9
EDUCATORS (224)	41	46	13
CUSTODY ADMINISTRATORS (350)	45	21	34
POLICY MAKERS (98)	48	28	24
SUPERVISORS OF FEMALES (67)	67	20	13
MAINTENANCE WORKERS (397)	68	17	15
CORRECTIONAL OFFICERS (1,470)	73	15	12
RESEARCHERS (15)	73		27
TECHNICIANS (259)	78	12	10
PHYSICIANS AND DENTISTS (47)	87	11	2
CLERICAL & OFFICE WORKERS (413)	95	3	2
TOTAL (3,654)	65	20	15

0 10 20 30 40 50 60 70 80 90 100
PERCENT

CHART 2

Percentages are based on the number of respondents in each category. Forty-eight, or slightly more than 1 per cent, did not answer this question. In no category of employees did the proportion of non-respondents exceed 4 per cent.
Group therapy and group counseling were combined in this chart.

nel. It is a treatment activity that can, over a period of time, reach most of the inmates. Group treatment in California prisons was widely viewed by administrators as good for everybody, or nearly everybody. In January, 1957, only about 1 per cent of the parolees leaving state prisons in California had one or more years of group counseling. In 1960, approximately 50 per cent had had group counseling.[1]

Groups were not always continuous. Fifteen per cent of all correctional employees who once led a treatment group were not doing so in January, 1959. There also were prisoners who dropped out of on-going groups for personal or administrative reasons. On July 1, 1960, 9,580 inmates were in counseling groups, however, and there were about 2,000 in group psychotherapy. The total represented more than half of the entire inmate population.

NEWISTIC ENTHUSIASM

Group treatment was more widespread in the California Department of Corrections in 1960 than in any other network of treatment institutions in the United States.[2] At the California Medical Facility at Vacaville, nearly all of the eligible inmates were in group psychotherapy or group counseling. At Tehachapi, group counseling has been compulsory for all inmates since 1956 as an experimental alternative to adding gun towers, perimeter fencing, an armory, and other security devices. These facilities, plus twenty-three custodial personnel to man them, would have cost $85,000 in capital outlay and over $100,000 a year for twenty-four hour maintenance. Tehachapi's incidence of escape is low in spite of the absence of many of the usual prison security devices. A senior official now gives much of the credit for this record to the group counseling program. He thought that "Before a guy hits the fence, he has to explain himself to 400 head shrinkers," fellow inmates acting like psychiatrists.

But what basis was there for organizational readiness in 1956 for a proposal made to scrap plans already drawn for building a

[1] These estimates were made by Robert M. Harrison, Departmental Supervisor of Group Counseling.

[2] Lloyd W. McCorkle and Albert Elias: "The Present Status of Group Psychotherapy in Correctional Institutions, *Federal Probation*, Vol. XXIV, No. 2, June, 1960.

fence and gun tower at Tehachapi? There was no evidence. But there was confidence in the effectiveness of group treatment, before it could be tested by research. Norman Fenton recalls that the decision to experiment was made quickly, after enthusiastic endorsement from every segment of the prison system:

> 2:30 P.M. — Talked the idea of 100 per cent group counseling over with Associate Superintendent Lloyd, who was in charge at Tehachapi. He agreed.
>
> 3:00 P.M. — Met with the Associate Superintendent's staff. They agreed.
>
> 4:00 P.M. — Met with the Inmate Advisory Council. They were favorable.
>
> 7:00 P.M. — The Associate Superintendent called his immediate administrative superior at Chino. He agreed to support the experiment.
>
> 7:30 P.M. — Met with an assembly of 300 inmates in the mess hall. They seemed cooperative.
>
> Next morning — Called Director Richard McGee and informed him of this widespread organizational support of the idea to experiment with 100 per cent group counseling in place of building gun towers and heavy fencing. He gave his approval immediately.[1]

The Department of Corrections has clearly defined channels of command. Orders are issued from the top and prompt compliance is expected from those in lower echelons. This authority structure is modified by an administrative preference that persons with power to issue orders consult with subordinates before adopting regulations. Not all orders emanating from headquarters are endorsed by lower echelon persons. Their suggestions often result in modification of policy. It is reasonable to infer that group counseling grew not only because the Department's Deputy Director favored it; he involved middle and lower level administrators as well as line staff and inmates in the consultation process. And there were many who favored the innovation and defended it against others who were more skeptical.

Even in 1959, when the group counseling program was no longer new and only sketchy research data were available to docu-

---

[1]From a personal communication by Norman Fenton, dated September 22, 1961.

ment its effectiveness, a majority of the employees expressed the opinion that group counseling had positive effects. About half of them thought that group counseling tends to bring about basic personality change in many offenders, reduces the incidence of rule violations by prison inmates, and improves the chances of getting early parole dates from the Adult Authority. Only 9 per cent agreed with the statement that "group counseling has no proven effects on anyone or anything." Sixty-three per cent thought this idea to be false and 26 per cent were *uncertain* (see Table 2).

This strong organizational commitment co-existed with widespread uncertainty about its relative effectiveness. Those admin-

TABLE 2

OPINIONS OF DEPARTMENT OF CORRECTIONS EMPLOYEES REGARDING THE EFFECTIVENESS
OF GROUP COUNSELING

(In Per Cent)

(N = 3,654)	True	Uncertain	False	No Response
Offenders in group counseling tend to break fewer prison rules than those who do not participate	52	35	11	2
Group counseling tends to bring about basic personality change in many offenders	51	13	34	2
Offenders in group counseling improve their chances of early parole by the Adult Authority	48	32	17	3
Staff people who volunteer to do group counseling with offenders improve their chances for promotion in the Department of Corrections	32	44	22	2
Offenders in group counseling are less likely to become recidivists than those who do not participate regularly	28	55	15	2
Group counseling brings correctional officers close to how prisoners feel. This interferes with their capacity to maintain proper discipline among offenders during regular custody duties	10	15	73	2
Group counseling has no proven effects on anyone or anything	9	26	63	2

TABLE 3

OPINION REGARDING THE ACTIVITY WHICH BEST HELPS IN THE REFORMING
OF PRISON INMATES*

(In Per Cent)

	Psycho-therapy	Group Counsel-ing	Educa-tion**	Imprison-ment and Loss of Civil Rights	Recrea-tion	No Response
Mental Health Personnel (N = 159)	63	3	11	21	***	2
Researchers (N = 15)	60	7	13	13	***	7
Chaplains (N = 22)	45	–	18	14	***	23
Policy Makers (N = 98)	44	7	16	31	***	2
Parole Officers (N = 130)	35	2	24	35	***	4
Educators (N = 227)	21	5	44	23	1	6
Supervisors of Females (N = 67)	21	7	34	38	***	***
Technicians (N = 259)	17	7	32	39	1	4
Physicians and Dentists (N = 47)	17	4	34	39	***	6
Clerical and Office Workers (N = 413)	16	6	38	36	***	4
Custody Administrators (N = 350)	14	4	30	50	***	2
Correctional Officers (N = 1,470)	10	5	33	44	3	5
Maintenance Workers (N = 397)	8	8	32	44	2	6
Total (N = 3,654)	17	6	31	40	1	5

*First choices in answer to the following question: "Many activities in a prison are undertaken to help the inmates. Please select the *three* which in your opinion tend to make the greatest impact on an offender's chance of reforming. Write number 1 next to your first choice, number 2 next to your second choice, and number 3 next to your third choice. Please rank only *three*."

**Combined first choices of vocational, academic, industrial, agricultural.

***Less than 1 per cent.

istratively responsible for expanding group treatment had been careful to make no claims that it would provide a panacea. Only 28 per cent of the Department's employees in 1959 thought that "Offenders in group counseling are less likely to become recidivist than those who do not participate regularly." Although group counseling was ranked first more often than group psychotherapy among activities judged to "make the greatest potential impact on a parolee's chance of reforming," both techniques made a poor showing in the importance imputed to them among alternate prison reformation methods (see Table 3). Only 6 per cent of all Departmental employees checked group counseling as making "the greatest impact on offenders" when given a choice of eight reform-oriented approaches. Similar skepticism was expressed with regard to its relative importance among alternate treatment approaches to parolees (see Table 4). Technicians, physicians, custody and maintenance employees express less confidence in the effectiveness of both forms of group treatment than vocational education and the punitive loss of freedom and civil rights.

What then accounts for the emergence of group counseling for special organizational encouragement among alternate prison and parole programs? Educational activities, particularly vocational and academic training and religious activities, were already established before group treatment ideas were ever thought of. Hundreds of full and part-time chaplains, teachers, and shop supervisors were employed to perform these alternate reform-oriented services. By what process did correctional officials (including many of the chaplains, teachers, and shop supervisors) come to take an interest in group treatment, a technique that was not part of their occupational specialties?

Interest in group treatment mushroomed beyond the Department of Corrections, in the California Department of the Youth Authority, in the Los Angeles County Probation Department, and in other California correctional jurisdictions, including some of the county and city jails, where persons awaiting trial and most of those convicted for misdemeanors are housed. And why was it that group counseling, rather than group psychotherapy, grew more rapidly although the latter is viewed as being more promising as a rehabilitation technique by professional authority figures?

TABLE 4

OPINION REGARDING THE ACTIVITY WHICH BEST HELPS IN THE REFORMING OF PAROLEES[1]
(In Per Cent)

	Psycho- therapy	Group Counsel- ing	Parole Officer Advice and Help	Surveil- lance Aspects of Parole	No Response
Researchers (N = 15)	40	20	20	20	—
Mental Health Personnel (N = 159)	23	6	51	19	1
Chaplains (N = 22)	14	18	41	18	9
Educators (N = 224)	12	14	48	18	8
Policy Makers (N = 98)	12	5	53	19	11
Physicians and Dentists (N = 47)	10	6	49	27	8
Technicians (N = 259)	8	10	58	19	5
Parole Officers (N = 130)	8	5	53	28	6
Supervisors of Females (N = 67)	4	13	67	9	7
Correctional Officers (N = 1,470)	4	8	48	31	9
Clerical and Office Workers (N = 413)	4	8	63	19	6
Custody Administrators (N = 350)	4	6	54	32	4
Maintenance Workers (N = 397)	3	13	44	29	11
Total (N = 3,654)	6	9	51	27	7

[1]First choices in answer to the following question: "Many activities in parole are undertaken as a means of reforming the parolee. Please select *three* of the following activities and programs which in your opinion make the greatest potential impact on an offender's chance of reforming. Write number 1 next to your first choice, number 2 next to your second choice and number 3 next to your third choice. Please rank only *three*." Seven alternatives were offered. To simplify data presentation in this table they were combined into four categories.

Psychotherapy at the Parole Outpatient Clinic.

Group counseling while on parole.

The advice and active help received from the parole officer in obtaining financial help, employment, housing, etc.

Offender's knowledge of being under surveillance and control of a parole officer.

The experience of parole hearing with the Adult Authority.

The ever present realization of the possibility of being placed in jail and/or returned to prison.

The fact of being expected to abide by a specific set of parole conditions symbolized by parolees signing a contract to this effect.

We shall now proceed to examine these questions in the social-historical context of a scientific reform movement, a collective enterprise to channel prevalent restlessness into planned action designed to bring about a desired condition.[1] Its emergence and current status will be described to show that it has the attributes of a scientific social movement in which faith in humanism and science co-exist. Its administrative leaders espouse the ideology of the American correctional movement. They have been at work for years to attain its objectives by means of long-range administrative planning.

---

[1]This definition draws on Herbert Blumer: "Collective Behavior," in Alfred McClung Lee, *Principles of Sociology*. New York, Barnes and Noble, Inc., 1946; and Rudolph Heberle: "Observations on the Sociology of Social Movements," *American Sociological Review*, Vol. 14, June, 1949.

Chapter 4

CRISIS

THE CRISIS PRECIPITATION OF REFORM

Bank robber Sampsell had a long record of notorious crimes. He had a sentence of fifteen years to life in Folsom Prison. As the son of a well-to-do merchant, his "spoilt brat" escapades made good newspaper copy. Sampsell made repeated efforts to escape from prison, including the manufacture of a home-made pistol. When it was discovered that while serving sentence he was able to spend occasional week-ends with a lady-friend in her San Francisco apartment, California newspaper headlines exploded.[1]

Governor Earl Warren, who as District Attorney of Alameda County had presented the people's case against Sampsell, used this scandal as a springboard for action. The incident dramatized the fact that though he had been Governor for nearly a year, he was without authority to intervene directly. The Governor knew that the administration of Folsom Prison had been generally lax and ineffective, but the warden and the Board of Prison Directors to whom he reported had been appointed for a definite term by the previous Governor.

The Sampsell incident dramatized the urgency of placing the State's penal system on a professionally sound basis. At a special session of the legislature, called in 1944, bills for fundamental reforms of the penal system were ready, having been drafted by members of Governor Warren's staff. The public furor aroused by this scandal was used as a signal to press for their immediate adoption. The prison reform legislation passed as Senate Bill No. 1. It established a new Department of Corrections, with centralized re-

---

[1]*Los Angeles Times,* Sunday, November 28, 1943, P. 1, and Monday, November 29, 1943, P. 1.

sponsibility and power to modernize its penal practices.[1]

Public officials are not free to introduce reforms as they see fit. Their power is derived from an official mandate. It is defined and restricted by law, custom, precedent, and inertia. Governor Warren had known for years that there was much in the California prisons system that was inefficient and corrupt. He did not have much legal authority over prison affairs. This in spite of his political power, as the state's chief executive, elected by a comfortable majority, and chief of his party with control of both houses of the State Legislature.

Crisis creates a public climate favorable to change by sensitizing segments of public opinion to the need for action. A crisis sanctions taking a new look at policies long taken for granted. Its drama paves the appearance of urgency, even though similar conditions may have been of long duration. In the busy lives of the average citizen, routine public affairs are given little attention. Only a dramatic incident calls attention to chronic problems that require a remedy.

Warren differed from his predecessors in California government in making a crisis out of what could have been treated as an embarrassing incident, to be explained away in order not to disturb the status quo. He had carefully prepared for change, however, by the drafting of detailed reform legislation. He seized upon the Sampsell case to arouse public opinion through newspaper and other publicity about the need for penal reform. This public interest in turn influenced a not entirely enthusiastic legislature to consider fundamental reform. The drama of the Sampsell scandal helped Warren to counteract efforts by some wardens and legislators to settle for a symbolic rather than a substantive break with past administrative practices.

Warren's legislative proposals dealt decisively with critical problems of correctional work with adults, that had plagued California since its establishment in 1851. Before the reform, California state prisons seemed to be functioning as advanced centers of criminal education, rather than as settings inducive to reflection and re-socialization. Their history was characterized by chronic public

---

[1]Earl Warren and Burdette J. Daniels: "California's New Penal System," *California Law Review*, Vol. 32, September, 1944.

dissatisfaction with intervals of indignation when scandals broke. This thought plagued both the more well-meaning and more inept officials responsible at various times for state penal policies.

Prisons are society's last resort to control anti-social or mentally ill men and women who cannot be controlled by other institutions of the social system—their family, their friends, reference groups, and moral restraints. As Tirey L. Ford, one-time Attorney General of California, whom Governor Pardee appointed to the State Board of Prison Directors in 1905, pointed out:

> The most difficult of all penological problems are those presented for solution to state prison authorities, where, after all others had failed, the final effort is made to reclaim a citizen and to remold a human character. After the home has failed, after the school has failed, after the church has failed, after the juvenile court has failed, after the reform school has failed, after probation has failed, and after organized society has branded him as a felon and a moral outcast, then the delinquent is received at the state prison, and a final effort is made by the prison authorities to cure the moral infirmities that have grown and multiplied through the preceding years.[1]

State prisons in California were not equipped to meet these social expectations. Although such tortures as mutilation and branding were no longer in vogue as they were still in other parts of the world, California prison conditions reflected a degree of neglect and administrative stagnation that was widespread in prisons throughout the country.

THE SOCIOLOGY OF CRUELTY

The prison system of California began in 1851 when the Legislature contracted with M. G. Vallajo and James M. Estell to house prisoners on a ship moored in San Pablo Bay. In return for full use of the prisoner labor, these two private entrepreneurs agreed to arrange for their safe-keeping, and security, and to provide them with food and clothing. This arrangement was to continue until the completion of San Quentin Prison in 1854 by inmate labor.[2]

---

[1] Tirey L. Ford: *California State Prisons: Their History, Development and Management.* San Francisco, The Star Press, 1910.

[2] The lease system for prisoners persisted in many states well into the 20th Century. It is still in vogue in some Southern states for inmates of county jails.

The lease arrangement, by which the labor of prisoners was contracted out by the State for financial consideration to private persons, was consistent with strongly prevailing public sentiments that criminals should not become a drain on the taxpayers. Near or complete budgetary self-sufficiency was viewed to be an important criterion of efficiency of a prison administrator.

During the early years of San Quentin, abuses and corruption often led to political controversy. In some cases prisoners were allowed to roam around the county, and a few were permitted to act as guards. Gambling and drinking were openly permitted within the prison walls. Pretty women prisoners were dispensing amatory favors. But there were many others who suffered tortures, including thumb stretching and terrible beatings. Less favored prisoners had no underwear and wore burlap bags on their feet.[1]

Extremes of punishment in prisons are generally associated with illicit rewards for prisoners who help the custodians do their work. As late as 1944, the head inmate male nurse at Folsom prison had prior narcotic convictions. He had a key to the dispensary and was allowed by the doctor, who was in part-time residence, to possess narcotics for administering to patients "in an emergency."[2] Inmates who could pay bribes or who did personal favors for certain staff people also could count on relief from some of the onerous conditions of prison life.

Without mutually shared goals there is no basis to nurture voluntary cooperation of persons in this caste system of free and inmate personnel. Inmates are incarcerated because they were caught while engaged in law violations. Most of them are ambivalent, if not opposed to many of the rules and expectations that are imposed by prison administrators in the name of the state. They are involuntarily part of a total institution in which the staff has most of the power and few restraints. The inmates have little power and many restraints.

---

[1] Paraphrased from Clinton T. Duffy: *San Quentin: The Story of a Prison*. London, Peter Davies, 1951.

[2] Julian H. Alco, Chairman, with Charles H. Deuel, Walter A. Gordon, Pierce H. Fazel, J. H. McClelland, and Burdette J. Daniels: *Preliminary Report of Governor's Committee on Penal Affairs: Folsom Prison and San Quentin Escapes on December 26, 1943*. Submitted to Honorable Earl Warren, Governor of California, Sacramento, California, March 10, 1944.

The restrictions of prison life are an ever-present inducement to corruption. Living conditions are austere, with few privileges. Prisoners are left on a minimum level of subsistence. They are removed from close interaction of persons whom they love. Heterosexual expressions of libidinal impulses are impossible. Contact of inmates with representatives of their society is largely restricted to their guards—free people differentiated from inmates in many ways. Few staff members associate with inmates in any personal way. Most of the rights and privileges enjoyed by free adults are being withheld from prisoners.

In spite of these irksome conditions, which help to make imprisonment a form of punishment, hardened and confirmed criminals often get along well. They do their time quietly in order to get it over with quickly. But they do not change. They make no gains in prison in capacity for self-control; they do not learn to get along in an acceptable fashion after their release. Ingenuity is required to motivate people incarcerated against their will to cooperate with their custodians in genuine efforts of inmate treatment and rehabilitation.

This complex problem of management was usually entrusted to persons unequal to it. Before 1944, California prison employees, at both managerial and operational levels, relied primarily on penalties to deter inmates from violating prison rules. Since most inmates serve indeterminate sentences, custodial officials can invite compliance because they have the power to delay an inmate's release. "Good time" credits, allowed for satisfactory behavior, can be taken away. For criminal violations, inmates can be tried and given an additional sentence. But if these major penalties were used to punish minor violations, few persons would ever qualify for parole. To enforce day-to-day routines, officials needed more immediate means to assert their control.

What means for control are available? If the prison fare is already austere what can be denied before resulting in undernourishment and starvation? If the small cell is already bare of conveniences, what can be removed to serve as punishment without resulting in the use of a San Quentin's infamous dungeon? If the sentence is already long, the prospects of earning one's release seem unreal.

The attempted solution to the problems of enforcing prison rules has often been to get "tough" and if need be, still "tougher" in spite of evidence that, when living conditions are too harsh, violence and riots are highly likely. Fear of revolt on the part of the prison keepers may justify in their eyes measures of "preventive" dehumanization. Inmates then are treated with less concern for their welfare than animals. This has happened throughout history in systems where absolute control was exercised over persons who were social outcasts. The propensity for abusive practices to enforce the expectations of the system of the inmates had led to condoning social disapproved practices, such as the torture of French students by French secret service agents in the same building in which fifteen years earlier the Nazi Gestapo has used torture to obtain information.[1] Even psychologically well-adjusted police interrogators are sometimes tempted to use force in order to get a suspect in a heinous crime to name his accomplices. The probability of atrocity is increased when law enforcement agencies employ persons who have sadistic tendencies and who derive deep satisfaction from exercising power. Prison work can be attractive to such persons.

When excessive cruelties and/or petty rackets come to the public's attention, those most directly responsible tend to be disciplined or fired. Occasionally, wardens and other prison officials have been dismissed for inefficiency, corruption, or gross abuse of inmates.[2] These personalized clean-up campaigns fail as lasting organizational remedies, however. They are focused on scandal prevention. They do not touch the underlying social forces in prison management that thrive on mediocrity and corruption, and rely on brutality and neglect to insure absolute control.

SPASMODIC REFORM

California's prisons have had their periodic scandals, but have

---

[1] Edward Rodity: "The Criminal as a Public Servant," *Commentary*, Vol. 28, November, 1959.

[2] Tirey L. Ford: *California State Prisons: Their History, Development and Management. Op. Cit.*; Milton Chermin: *A History of California State Administration in the Field of Penology.* Berkeley, California, University of California, Masters dissertation, submitted in 1929; Frank Bobby William Hawkinshire, V.: *A History of the California Department of Corrections, 1944-1959.* Berkeley, California, University of California, Masters dissertation, submitted in 1959.

never been without employees who espoused humane sentiments. Their accomplishments were temporary and personal rather than organizational. Their reforms usually resigned or died with them, for only rarely was a thoughtful guard, warden, or prison director replaced by a person of equal stature.

As early as 1858, a California Legislative Committee urged comprehensive reforms. Several subsequent legislative reports proposed policies which would even now be accepted as a "model" by many of the country's penologists. In 1879, a constitutional amendment went into effect designed to take the prison system out of party politics. It provided for a Board of five prison directors, each to serve for ten years. They had staggered terms. Appointments were to be made by the Governor with the advice and consent of the Senate. No governor could make more than two appointments during any four-year term of office, unless vacancies occurred due to death, resignation, or malfeasance in office by an incumbent Board member. This Board, rather than the Governor, had power to appoint wardens, physicians, clerks, and other prison personnel. Nevertheless, in 1903, a legislative committee complained that California prisons were "schools of vice and universities of crime." The majority objected to the then prevalent tendency to blame particular individuals. Rather they expressed the view:

> "The responsibility for this great wrong rests primarily not
> with the wardens, nor yet with the Board of Prison Directors, but
> upon the people of California who have followed a false idea of
> economy and, steeped in neglect of public affairs, have failed to
> provide the means for the proper conduct of these institutions."[1]

Efforts to reform inmates were restricted to spiritual exhortation and some educational activities. California was among the states that proudly reported in 1868 to be conducting "the experiment of a school." There were 20 classes with 160 students, each taught to read and write by one or more of the literate convicts.

The public, then and now, looks upon inmates in terms of multiple explanatory models. Inmates may be viewed as primarily

---

[1] *Journal of the Assembly,* 35th Session of the Legislature of the State of California, 1903, "Report of the Select Committee on State Prisons and Reformatory Institutions," Sacramento, California, March 10, 1903.

sick and socially deprived persons in need of help; they may be regarded as bad and dangerous, in need of control and punishment. Often they are also thought of being defective degenerates, requiring custodial care to protect society from their otherwise uncontrollable depravities. Prisons have to be managed in terms of these quite contradictory theories.

Their co-existence has always made it difficult for prison employees to know when they were pursuing the "right" policy.[1] There is no single mandate for what prisons should accomplish. There is strong political sanction for the point of view that criminals should be punished for their crimes, but at the same time, there is great readiness to vary such punishment on the basis of the offender's personal characteristics and his avowed willingness to do penitence and to improve.

The reform point of view has sometimes won out because it is good business. A work therapy program might serve business interests by providing cheap labor. One contractor who made bricks in San Quentin conceived the idea of replacing his free employees with prisoners close to their being discharged. The prison directors allowed the contractor to credit the convicts with half the wages he would have had to pay to the free personnel. For inmates, the wages —even reduced—were a strong incentive because they were enabled to accumulate money while in prison for the time when they would be freed. At the same time, this practice reduced the contractor's costs.

FORCES FAVORING MEDIOCRITY

Law enforcement and the administration of justice are primarily a local responsibility. Except for Federal crimes, jurisdiction over the care and supervision of criminals is at the county and state level. Reforms in one county or state do not affect neighboring jurisdictions. Jealously guarded local autonomy makes it difficult for any national effort to be generally effective. To bring about a general penal reform, it would be necessary to arouse a group of interested citizens in each and every locality. Citizen groups are

---

[1]Donald R. Cressey: "Contradictory Directives in Complex Organizations: The Case of the Prison," *Administrative Science Quarterly*, Vol. 4, June, 1959.

more likely to make a mark at the state level when they can rely on a large cadre of qualified governmental specialists, to whom planned administrative change is not only a job but a calling that has spiritual meaning for them.

Between 1851 and 1944, a number of important legislative reforms were introduced in the California system. Indeterminate sentences and parole were adopted. The first forestry camp was set up in 1915. But the overall administration orientation of the Department was vacillating. Reform ideas had a precarious and spasmodic effect on the system. No element in the citizenry was consistent in supporting them. Prisoners do not vote. No powerful legislative lobby favored modernization of prison conditions. Taxpayer groups were opposed to anything that would greatly add to costs. Like many other public institutions, prisons were used by politicians to provide jobs for friends. Professionalization of prison management would do away with this source of patronage. Members of the legislature who were lawyers had a source of influence when representing inmates or their relatives in petitions for parole or pardon.

Prison administrators like all civil servants tend to be praised if they save money. In prisons, economy was often accomplished by reducing the comforts and living standards of the inmates, who could not easily protest. Prisons are not alone among total institutions where there is an economic incentive for the toleration of such unsatisfactory conditions. Orphanages, hospitals for the mentally ill, and the retarded also are often administered with more concern for economy than quality of services. But prisons, which deal with a very unpopular category of deviants, are particularly prone to be under-financed. Those in California were nearly always overcrowded—too many prisoners, too few employees and the legislature was slow to expand facilities as the prison population increased.

The rewards were meager for working in such a conflict-ridden and, sometimes, physically dangerous field of management. Correctional salaries were low in California, as elsewhere in America.[1]

---

[1]Gresham M. Sykes: *The Society of Captives: A Study of Maximum Security Prisons.* Princeton, Princeton University Press, 1958. Attention is called to the fact that more than 50 per cent of the guards were temporarily employed who had not passed a Civil Service examination.

Guards have the closest, most extensive, and longest-range contact with the offenders. But their organizational status is quite low. Employees closely identified with medical and psychosocial treatment—doctors, social workers, psychologists, educators, and chaplains—were more highly regarded and much better paid than those primarily concerned with custody—although the officers supervising cell blocks or manning guard towers are necessary to keep order; treatment people could be dispensed with.

Some of those willing to make a career in the correctional field derived satisfactions from the exercise of absolute control over people and were sadistic or psychosexually deviant. The fact that such perverts may be quite efficient made it unlikely for them to be weeded out. The borderline is not easily drawn between cruelty and just "being tough" with criminals, especially those who periodically frighten prison officials and the public alike with riots or acts of violence within the prison.[1]

It was rare for prisons to retain their more qualified younger recruits. A sort of Gresham's Law seemed to be operative in which pathological and rigid employees drove out of prison work those with more idealistic motivations. Being good, they could more easily find alternate employment than the least qualified employees. Unsatisfactory working conditions that persist over a long period of time tend to select marginal workers who have no choice but to put up with them.

Prison conditions in California until the 1930's were characterized by the ebb and flow of a chronic crisis. Its roots were widely recognized. Those responsible for law enforcement and prison work included some who opposed the *status quo* as being out of harmony with correctional reform ideals. Lay public opinion forces favorable to change were mobilized by periodic scandals. Their regular recurrence reduced the prestige of vested interests supportive of the old order. They were on the defensive. The stage was set for a fundamental reorganization of the prison system.

---

[1]Between 1950 and April, 1958, there were 105 riots or serious disturbances in American prisons, including some of those with advanced penological practices. See Donald R. Clemmer: *The Prison Community.* New York, Rinehart and Company, 1958; see also Austin H. MacCormick: "Behind the Prison Riots," *The Annals of the American Academy of Political and Social Science,* Vol. 53, May, 1954.

This is what happened in 1944, when a statewide unified Department of Corrections was organized in California. It espoused few unique or new ideas. Most of them were like those promulgated by the first American Prison Congress in 1870. California, however, built a stable legislative and administrative framework in which these long-cherished reform standards could be tried out under conditions favorable to their effective realization.

Chapter 5

INCUBATION

Dissatisfaction with prison conditions was nation-wide. But so were forces that supported the continuation of unsatisfactory practices. Political selection of personnel was the rule rather than exception in state prisons. In the 1930's, most states were without a civil service commission. While there was one in California, the commission there had no jurisdiction over posts in penal or correctional institutions. There had been little change in penological personnel practices since 1870; the latter were reported by Frederick Howard Wines in 1895:

> The state of American prisons twenty-five years ago was far from satisfactory. The discipline in most of them was either severe to the verge of cruelty, or lax to the point of weakness, according to the ideas and sentiments of the wardens in charge. The wardens were appointed almost wholly for political reasons, and were subject to change with every alteration in the political complexion of the State governments. Comparatively few of them were really competent for their position, and they did not, as a rule, remain in office long enough to become thoroughly acquainted with their duties and qualified to perform them. The majority of them openly professed a disbelief in the possibility of convict reformation.[1]

NATIONAL REFORM EFFORTS

There was a difference in the reform efforts of the late 1920's and the 1930's and those of earlier periods. They went beyond scandal prevention. They did not rely only on emotional appeal to citizens to rally against occasional reprehensible abuses of in-

---

[1]Frederick H. Wines: *Punishment and Reformation.* New York, Thomas Y. Crowell Company, 1923.

mates or the corruption of prison personnel. Reform proceeded from organized research resulting in detailed technical proposals of what might be tried to reform the entire prison system. For instance, a group of lawyers in Missouri collected funds for a fundamental survey of how the Missouri state government dealt with law enforcement and crime control. It took note of failings of individuals, but went beyond them to indicate that reform could not endure without a supportive organizational structure. Missouri served as a case study of penological questions that were national and international in scope.[1]

In 1929, when Herbert Hoover became President, his newly appointed Attorney General, William Dewitt Mitchell, held the view that the "prison situation presented one of the major problems that the Department of Justice would have to deal with" during his incumbency.[2] Careful studies of general policies were undertaken. They provided the technical bases for a comprehensive administration reorganization.[3] A unified Federal Bureau of Prisons was set up. Congress approved a policy of facilitating more individualized treatment of different categories of inmates:

> It is hereby declared to be the policy of the Congress that institutions be so planned and limited in size as to facilitate the development of an integrated, federal and penal correctional system which will assure the proper classification and segregation of federal prisoners according to their character, the nature of the crime they have committed, their mental conditions and such other factors that should be taken into consideration in providing

---

[1]The Missouri Association for Criminal Justice, *The Missouri Crime Survey*. New York, Macmillan and Company, 1926. While the report did not deal with prisons, it studied the machinery that brought men there and examined the administration of paroles, pardons and commutation.

[2]Statement of Honorable William Dewitt Mitchell, Attorney General of the United States, "Federal Prisoners and Penitentiaries," *Hearings Before the Committee on the Judiciary, United States Congress, House of Representatives*, 71st Congress, 2nd session, on H. R. 6807, H. R. 7410, H. R. 7411, H. R. 7412, H. R. 7413 and H. R. 7832, December 19, 1929, Serial I. Washington, United States Government Printing Office, 1929.

[3]"Federal Penal and Reformatory Institutions," *Hearings Before the United States House, the Special Committee on Penal and Reformatory Institutions*, 70th Congress, 2nd session, pursuant to House Resolution 233, 70th Congress, 1st session, January 7, 1929 to January 15, 1929. United States Government Printing Office, Washington, D. C., 1929.

an individualized system of discipline, care and treatment of persons committed to such institutions.[1]

Part of the administrative reform was to provide for a professionalized work force. In 1930, untrained guards worked for ten hours a day, seven days a week. They were replaced gradually by specialized and technically trained personnel. By 1955, all federal wardens, associate wardens, and the heads of the various institutional services were career officers, without political obligations to anyone.

The call to lead the Federal Bureau of Prisons went to Sanford Bates, head of the Department of Corrections of Massachusetts and a former president of the American Prison Association (1926-27). This experience had given him an historical and world-wide perspective on correctional reform efforts. He was one of those responsible in 1930 for revision and reaffirmation by the American Prison Association of the principles adopted by the First congress in 1870.[2] Bates attracted (as Deputy Director) James V. Bennett, of the Federal Bureau of Efficiency, who had written several key congressional reports that led to the legislative reform of the prison system. The task of developing educational and social welfare programs was turned over to Austin H. MacCormick.[3] All three of these persons were later part of the supporting cast of national correctional reform leaders, who encouraged similar, and in some ways, more extensive penal reform efforts in California.

The Federal prison system was born during the depth of the "Great Depression." Jobs were scarce. Young men with vision had more limited vocational opportunities than they had before or since. The Federal prison system offered more than a job. It also espoused a cause: penal reform. It was able to attract and keep a cadre of young career professionals. Among them was Richard A. McGee, later to become the Director of the California Department of Corrections.

---

[1]*Federal Prisons, 1955,* Leavenworth, Kansas, United States Penitentiary, 1956.

[2]Sanford Bates: *Prisons and Beyond.* New York, The Macmillan Company, 1936.

[3]Austin H. MacCormick: *The Education of Adult Prisoners, A Survey and a Program.* New York, The National Society of Penal Information, 1931.

PRISON SYSTEM RESEARCH

Criminology was growing as a subject of empirical study in many universities. Thousands of students took courses in the field, and some of them went into prison work. Empirical research, done on many prison problems, reduced the areas where guesses took the place of knowledge. Special attention was given to these studies in the Sociology Departments of the University of Chicago, the University of Pennsylvania, and Indiana University. A growing pool of trained specialists thus became available. Some of them made a career in prison work, not simply to make a living, but also because they hoped to find there an opportunity to deal with a major social problem in a scientific manner.

In the early 1930's, the Bureau of Social Hygiene in New York commissioned a distinguished legal scholar and a professor of sociology to make a formal survey of the field of criminology to determine "whether or not it is desirable to establish an institute of criminology and of criminal justice." To answer this question, Jerome Michael and Mortimer J. Adler undertook to examine and to evaluate the field's state of knowledge in relevant methods of research. Taking a broad view of their mission, they included in their report an "analysis of the nature of empirical sciences and its differentiation from different kinds of knowledge; a consideration of the various practical problems engendered by the phenomenon of crime; the separation of the field of criminology from that of criminal justice in terms of the kind of knowledge needed to resolve their respective problems; and, finally, a definition of the theoretical problem of the criminal law, in the light of which the different bodies of knowledge which are useful to the legislator and the judge could be properly related and subordinated."[1]

A few years later, the Social Science Research Council sponsored a more sociologically-oriented research planning venture, imaginatively executed by Thorston Sellin.

While more than two decades have passed since the writing of these reports, neither is outdated. There have been many new studies in the field of criminology—"a bastard science grown out

---

[1]Jerome Michael and Mortimer J. Adler: *Crime, Law and Social Science.* New York, Harcourt, Brace and Company, 1933.

of public preoccupation with a social plague,"[1] to use Sellin's picturesque characterization of the body of knowledge regarding crime as a social phenomenon. Some of the knowledge obtained about its etiology, its identification, control, repression, treatment, and prevention has been applied spasmodically. But the questions of theory and methodology discussed by Professors Michael, Adler, and Sellin are as meaningful for today's research planning as they were when committed to print.

Beginning with 1925, the Osborne Association in New York began to issue reports on the state of prisons in various parts of the country. The reports were based in large measure on inspection by the Association's staff. Actual conditions were candidly related to the Association's standards, which generally were the same as the *Declaration of Principles*. In 1942 the Association published a detailed report on every California Federal and State prison. Reform activities were already in ascendancy, but the spotlight of publicity may have helped to motivate officials to discontinue such practices as the use of disciplinary segregation cells, without modern conveniences, the use of striped prison clothing and to allow inmates to receive California newspapers. In its published report, the Osborne Association staff was able to report these changes in footnotes to the description of conditions at the time when the field study had been made.[2]

TECHNICAL PREPARATIONS IN CALIFORNIA

Research and planning for penal reform also began in California during the 1930's. The administrative problems that had plagued the prisons of the State since its establishment were actually less acute than they had been in earlier years, but more demanding standards of governmental operations made them less tolerable. The "warehousing" philosophy of old line custodians was being more and more questioned by advocates of the point of view that good custody was based on firm, but fair, humane, and efficient

[1] Thorsten Sellin: *Culture, Conflict and Crime*. New York, Social Science Research Council, 1938, Bulletin.

[2] Austin H. MacCormick (Editor): *Handbook of American Prisons and Reformatories*, Vol. II, Pacific Coast States, Fifth Edition. New York, The Osborne Association, Inc., 1942.

administration, which could command the respect of the inmates and the public alike.

The Bureau of Public Administration of the University of California at Berkeley, with a grant from the Rockefeller Foundation, sponsored a number of technical studies on the administration of criminal justice. Highlighted were such problems as the overcrowding of prisons, the inadequacy of classification of inmates, the insufficiency of work experiences for inmates, the absence of civil service regulations, and the inefficiency of general administration.[1]

A graduate seminar was held at the University of California in Berkeley in the 1930's, dealing with problems of the administration of justice. Among the guest lecturers was the young District Attorney of Alameda County, Earl Warren. He showed an interest in the use of science in criminology long before his election to the governorship in 1942 made it possible for him to sponsor penal reform actions at the state level. The seminar's coordinator was Dr. Milton Chernin, whose Master's dissertation was *A History of California State Administration in the Field of Penology*. It endorsed an administrative model patterned after the almost forgotten Cincinnati resolutions of the first Congress of Correction in 1870 by reviving specific suggestions published more than a decade earlier by Stuart A. Queen, a sociologist and Secretary of the California State Board of Charities and Corrections from 1913 to 1917.

> Courts would determine the question of guilt or innocence and commit the violator to the executive board for an indefinite period, sending him to one of the central clearing houses. (One would probably be in San Francisco and one in Los Angeles.) There he would undergo a thorough physical, mental and psychoanalytical examination. He would be observed for several weeks and receive the necessary medical treatment. Criminal

---

[1]Earl Warren and Burdette J. Daniels: "California's New Penal System," *California Law Review*, Vol. 32, September, 1944. Recommendations to streamline administrative authority were cited as having been made by: Milton Chernin, "Legislative Problem No. 17," Bureau of Public Administration, University of California, Berkeley, December 15, 1934; Governor's Committee for Investigation of Penal Institutions, State of California, Sacramento, Report of the Committee on State Organization to the Governor and Legislature, State of California, Sacramento, 1941; Milton Chernin, "Legislative Problem No. 6," Bureau of Public Administration, University of California, Berkeley, 1941.

identification and special investigation into his past would, meantime, be made by expert caseworkers. With the reports of all these examinations in his hand, the superintendent of the clearing house would send the man to the institution best suited to his needs. He would send the manager of this institution a complete report of the man's social history, his physical and mental condition, with suggestions for proper treatment. The man would then receive the most intelligent treatment possible to restore him to normal citizenship. If conditions warrant it, he could be transferred to a different institution. If found mentally defective, he would probably never be released. When ready for a measure of freedom, he would be paroled, and if he made good, would finally be released.[1]

In the early 1940's, these humanitarian treatment ideas had attained the support of most criminologists and were also espoused by prominent persons in both major political parties. They were soon to be implemented, but in 1930, Chernin had much reason to exclaim: "This plan sounds Utopian, but there is nothing impossible in its realization."[2]

JUVENILE REFORM PRECEDENTS

In California, as elsewhere in the world, it was easier to get public support for a humanistic approach to juvenile rather than to adult offenders. Public receptivity for changes in the treatment of adult offenders, however, was increased by these precedents in the use of therapy-oriented policies for juvenile delinquents.

An early foreshadowing of this change in basic orientation, from a control to an education and treatment emphasis, was a decision by the California Legislature in 1921 to redefine the theoretical objectives of Whittier State School, then in existence for thirty years.

1891. Purpose: " . . . discipline, education, employment, reformation and protection of juvenile delinquents."

1921. Purpose: "There shall be established and maintained

---

[1]Milton Chernin: *A History of the California State Administration in the Field of Penology.* Berkeley, California, The University of California, Master's dissertation in Political Science, 1930; paraphrased from Stuart A. Queen: *The Passing of the County Jail.* Menosha, Wisconsin, The Collegiate Press, 1920.

[2]*Ibid.*: 237.

in this State a junior state school, an educational institution for boys in need of education, training, care, supervision and moral development therein provided."[1]

Even earlier, in 1917, the California Legislature had authorized the establishment of a California Bureau for Juvenile Research. The proposal was patterned after the then well-known Ohio Bureau of the same name, which provided diagnostic and treatment services for problem children. Not until 1928, when the Legislature appropriated $30,000, could the Bureau of Juvenile Research get beyond the blueprint stage. Dr. Norman Fenton, a clinical psychologist, was appointed as its Director. He and a staff of two psychiatric social workers and a psychiatrist administered psychological tests and offered counseling to selected children in correctional schools. In 1929, a demonstration program of traveling child guidance clinics was begun, modeled after a similar program in Illinois. Cases were selected as demonstrations on the basis of the following pattern:

1. A written request for help on a particular child's problems from a professional or lay person in a locality.
2. Assurance of local collaboration in the study of the child. (His case record was supplemented by first-hand study by a member of the staff of the Bureau of Juvenile Research before the problem was discussed at a diagnostic conference.)
3. Participation in the demonstration diagnostic conference of probation officers, teachers, and lay persons who were significantly related to the child's treatment.

The State Legislature drastically reduced the Bureau's annual appropriation in 1933 by 75 per cent to $7,500 a year. Fenton met this crisis by working only half time. He used the remaining $5,000 to supplement the salaries of a few clinical psychologists and social workers, employed in part-time service in state mental hospitals,

---

[1]Norman Fenton, with the collaboration of Jesse C. Fenton, Margaret E. Murray and Dorothy K. Tyson, *The Delinquent Boy in the Correctional School.* Claremont, California, Claremont College Guidance Center, 1935. Dr. Fenton points out that there have been analogies in this transition of names and purposes in other juvenile institutions. For example, the name of the New York Juvenile Asylum was changed to the Children's Village in 1920.

in return for their services as consultants on problem children. This improvisation made possible the continuation of limited child guidance services, at least in a number of localities.[1] The pattern of using available institutional staff to keep the program going rather than forlornly waiting for appropriations to hire full-time personnel was an expedient to be repeated later when Dr. Fenton started the group counseling program in California prisons.

The treatment point of view in the field of juvenile justice was further encouraged by the work of the American Law Institute. It had sponsored a two-year study of legislation on juvenile delinquency by its committee on *Criminal Justice: Youth*. About 200 experienced consultants from all parts of the nation participated. The result was a Model Youth Authority Corrections Act

" . . . based on the principle that the primary object of criminal justice is the protection of society. It embodies the principle of the indeterminate sentence. It seeks to make possible the application of our present knowledge of criminal behavior to the character and duration of correctional treatment for convicted youths. While not denying the therapeutic value for many delinquents of punishment, the Committee nevertheless believes that a specially qualified agency must determine the treatment best fitted to the individual, if he is to be regenerated and made safe to return to society. Hence the Model Act calls for the creation of a state authority to fill this obligation."[2]

The California Prison Association called a state-wide conference within a few months after the publication of the Model Act for California. Nearly two hundred judges, lawyers, educators, editors, ministers, prison administrators, probation officers, government officials, psychiatrists, sociologists, social workers, and representatives of civic organizations and clubs met to consider the Act's merits for California. After wide discussion from the floor, the conference unanimously endorsed it as a sentencing procedure. A

---

[1]J. H. Williams: "Early History of the California Bureau of Juvenile Research," *Journal of Juvenile Research*, Vol. 18, 1934; Norman Fenton, *State Child Guidance Service in California Communities*, Sacramento, California, Supervisor of Documents, Works Progress Administration 3257. Official Project 65-3-4183, 1938.

[2]American Law Institute: *State Action of the Model Youth Correction Authority Act*. Philadelphia, November, 1941.

state-wide committee was appointed to get these features adopted by the Legislature.

The conference was followed by much public discussion. For instance, by the summer of 1941, chapters of the California Federation of Women's Clubs had held fifty-four study conferences about the Model Act and the present California program. When it came to the floor of the Legislature, practically every major paper in the State published editorials endorsing it. The Act passed the Assembly unanmiously, and the Senate with only two dissenting votes.

Correctional reform thus attained the status of being a "nonpartisan" cause. But its administrative implementation was not. A highly regarded professional, Karl Holton, was appointed to head the new Youth Authority, but the Legislature appropriated only $100,000 for its work. The Legislature was under Republican control and reluctant to give the Democratic Governor, Culbert L. Olson, too much authority to develop extensive and expensive new treatment programs. This authority was subsequently granted during the administration of Governor Olson's Republican successor, Earl Warren.[1]

THE REFORM THAT STALLED

Public opinion was prepared for needed prison reform under the administration of Culbert L. Olson (1938 to 1942), the first Democrat to be elected Governor since the turn of the century. Elected with him, as Attorney General, was the Republican, Earl Warren. They did not work together well, although both showed many liberal ideas, including a dedicated interest for penal reform. Indicative of this concern was Warren's first act in office:

> "I decided to behave like a new broom on my first day as Attorney General," related Warren to Irving Stone, "and got to the office at 9 o'clock sharp.

---

[1]Robert E. Burke: *Olson's New Deal for California*. Berkeley and Los Angeles, University of California Press, 1953, especially p. 233. Many years after Governor Olson's defeat by Earl Warren in 1942, a popular story circulated in Sacramento in which conservatives were said to complain that their "chief difficulty with Earl Warren stemmed from the fact that Olson had departed without cleaning out the governor's desk!" Earl Warren had the political support and administrative skill to put into effect many ideas proposed by persons in Governor Olson's administration. One such idea was the proposal to expand the Youth Authority into a viable organization with adequate State funds.

Arriving there, he found two telephone messages, one of which informed him that the retiring Republican Governor Merriam's personal secretary had been selling pardons to San Quentin and Folsom prisoners on a cash basis, the second telling him that this devious gentleman had been appointed to the California bench by Merriam only the night before. By 9:15, Warren had the miscreant in his office, and he was taking the deposition which not only kept the man from becoming a judge, but led to his subsequent conviction.

Warren had promised a non-partisan regime, but this instantaneous fulfillment left the State gasping. One editor chuckled, "It is now going to be difficult to distinguish between Republican misdemeanors and Democratic torts."[1]

Governor Olson initiated an investigation of prison administrative practices. Its findings led him to fire the entire State Board of Prison Directors for toleration of corruption and mismanagement. Critics wondered if this action might not have been motivated also by political considerations. Prison jobs had been filled during prior Republican regimes with politically influential, but often incompetent persons. A new State Board of Prisons appointed by the Democrats would give this party an area for patronage, since most other state agencies were already covered by Civil Service Regulations. Political pressure was employed in some of the new appointments, but the key policy makers on the new Board of Prison Directors were persons dedicated to the cause of penal reform. Under the leadership of the chairman, Isaac Pacht, a former Los Angeles Superior Court Judge, several technically competent correctional officials were appointed to key posts. Clinton T. Duffy was made Warden of San Quentin, Kenyon Scudder, who had been in the forefront of the penal reform movement in California, was asked to become Superintendent of the State's newest penal institution at Chino. He was supported in resisting pressures (even when originating from Governor Olson's office) to hire personnel on the basis of political considerations. Although there were 2,300 applicants, Scudder was allowed to recruit a cadre of fifty young men on the basis of merit alone. Most of them had college degrees.

---

[1]Irving Stone: *Earl Warren: A Great American Story*. New York, Prentice-Hall, Inc., 1948.

Only one had ever worked in a prison before he was hired. The job that was defined to them was to establish a prison dedicated to rehabilitation rather than mere custody. These reform-oriented employees of the California Institution for Men were to have a major impact on the entire prison system. Many of them rose to positions of influence in the Department of Corrections or other State correctional agencies.[1]

Under Governor Olson, as on many previous occasions in California, prison reform was thought of in *personal* terms, the placement of qualified and well motivated persons in positions of leadership. No steps were taken to remedy fundamental administrative anachronisms. For instance, the reformed Board of Prison Directors was, like its predecessors, unpaid and part-time. Such a group was supposed to exercise over-all control. Its members could not give sufficient time to this task. During a two year period, the Board met for a total of 162 hours and 10 minutes in official meetings to administer "three prisons representing a capital investment of $10,386,710.90, with a total biennial budget of $5,000,000, with a staff of 600 paid personnel, with an average daily inmate population of 5,515 . . . "[2]

THE REFORM PROCEEDS

After Attorney General Warren became Governor in 1943, he asked for fundamental reorganization of the State's administrative structure in the correctional field, which had remained basically unchanged between 1879 and 1944. An integrated correctional

[1] The "Chino Pioneers," as these people are now called, meet annually for dinner. Membership in this group confers upon the individual the "halo" of having been through it all "from the beginning." The men who were hired at Chino are conscious of the fact that they experienced (and helped to make the experience) a drastic change in outlook in the California correction field. At the 1960 meetings, Walter Dunbar, the Department's Deputy Director, a "Chino Pioneer" himself, referred to the fact that children of the Chino pioneers were now beginning to make their careers in the correctional field. He became the Department's Director in October, 1961.

[2] Julian H. Alco, Chairman, with Charles H. Deuel, Walter A. Gordon, Pierce H. Fazel, J. H. McClelland and Burdette J. Daniels: *Preliminary Report of Governor's Committee on Penal Affairs: Folsom Prison and San Quentin Escapes on December 26, 1943.* Submitted to Honorable Earl Warren, Governor of California, Sacramento, California, March 10, 1944.

system came into being, in large part due to the following circumstances:

1. A favorable climate of public opinion had come into existence. The humanistic approach in penology enjoyed more acceptance than in prior periods.

2. The Governor of the State, Earl Warren, was a professional in the law enforcement field. He had strong convictions about the necessity of major "surgery" of the penal system. He had much technical knowledge about the problems that needed to be remedied. As a Republican Governor, with a Republican majority in both houses of the Legislature, he was able to exercise political leadership to implement a fundamental reform program.

3. Reform legislation was introduced after careful technical preparation. The Governor's secretary, Burdette Daniels, was assigned responsibility for revising and adapting to California conditions a legislative proposal that had been prepared for the reorganization of the Federal prison system. While Congress declined to enact many of these proposals for the Federal prison system, they were enacted into the laws of California.

4. The State had money to implement administrative reforms. World War II put an end to the State's budgetary stringency. Income from taxes was far in excess of expenditures.

5. Vested interests in the old order of the prison system were deprived of key incentives to favor its perpetuation. The prison system was taken out of politics. It was made illegal for lawyers to receive pay in any proceedings to obtain a parole or pardon.[1] The Governor was uncompromising in insisting that provisions be included to accomplish the end of the spoil system and to have one integrated prison administration headed by a full-time technician rather than a board. All employees other than the Director and a few other exempt positions were placed under Civil Service. Even the Director, who serves at the pleasure of the Governor, could be removed only after a public hearing.

6. The administration of the prison system was streamlined by providing for a single Director of Corrections. He was given responsibility to exercise power that had been lodged previously in three different boards appointed by the Governor but not dependent on him. They were the Board of Prison Directors, to

---

[1]*California Statutes,* 1943, Chapter 943, Paragraphs 2 and 3.

supervise the prisons; the Board of Prison Terms and Paroles; and the Advisory Pardon Board. While individuals who served on these boards included many public spirited citizens, their political positions often involved them in conflicts of power. Each of the members was likely to have influential backers.

7. The Director of Corrections was given full authority over the wardens who previously had been largely autonomous. A line organization was established in place of an anarchistic division of responsibility in which no one could effectively plan for reform because the power to do so was dissipated in so many ways.

The wardens lobbied strongly to keep their autonomy. But they were brought under the unquestioned administrative authority of the Director of Corrections. He alone was authorized to deal directly with the Governor and the Legislature, in line with the administrative centralization principle enunciated by the 1870 Congress of Corrections:

XXXVI. As a principle that crowns all, and is essential to all, it is our conviction that no prison system can be perfect, or even successful to the most desirable degree, without some central authority to sit at the helm, guiding, controlling, unifying and vitalizing the whole. We ardently hope yet to see all the departments of our preventive, reformatory and penal institutions in each state moulded into one harmonious and effective system; its parts mutually answering to and supporting each other; and the whole animated by the same spirit, aiming at the same objects, and subject to the same control; yet without loss of the advantages of voluntary aid and effort, wherever they are attainable.[1]

These political and administrative realities provided a backdrop for the emergence in California of penal treatment programs, including group counseling. A favorable political, fiscal and social climate had been emerging gradually, but there was no leadership to guide it decisively toward penal reform. Under Governor Earl Warren, an administrative crisis as old as California's statehood was resolved by reorganizing the entire state prison system.[2] Its

[1]Amercian Prison Association: "Declaration of Principles," *Proceedings of the 60th Annual Congress,* 1930.

[2]Earl Warren: "California Sentencing and Correctional Methods," in *The Public Papers of Chief Justice Earl Warren,* ed. Henry II. Christman (New York, Simon and Schuster, 1959). An address to the National Convention of the American Bar Association, Section on Criminal Law, Atlantic City, New Jersey, October 29, 1946.

direction was turned over to technicians with the mandate: more than safekeeping of inmates under humane conditions is needed; do also what is possible to reform prisoners during their period of incarceration. A new program had to be devised to meet this expectation.

APPOINTMENT OF A REFORM ADMINISTRATOR

VI. The two master forces opposed to the reform of the prison systems of our several states are political appointments, and a constant instability of administration. Until both are eliminated, the needed reforms are impossible.[1]

Governor Warren's selection of a Director of Corrections for his newly organized Department was very much in the spirit of this principle of the correctional reform movement. He decided to fill his Corrections cabinet post on the basis of a nation-wide civil service examination.

Notices were widely distributed inviting applications from anywhere in the United States. Applicants had to have a minimum of eight years of successful full-time paid employment in penal or correctional work that involved administrative responsibility of progressively increasing scope, including direction of two or more units with diverse activities. Written examinations were administered in Sacramento, San Francisco, Los Angeles, and other places throughout the United States as the number of candidates warranted. Those who passed were then invited to come to California for an oral examination.

Governor Warren appointed a professionally dominated selection panel. Its Chairman was James V. Bennett, Director of the Federal Bureau of Prisons. He was aided by a panel including Sanford Bates, Commissioner of the Board of Paroles of New York and then President of the American Parole Association, along with Justin Miller, Associate Justice of the United States District Court of Appeals in San Francisco, plus the Chairman of the California Personnel Board, or someone designated by him.

There were forty-nine applicants for the post. Twenty were

---

[1]American Prison Association: "Declaration of Principles," *Proceedings of the 60th Annual Congress,* 1930.

rejected for being beyond the age limit or lacking the necessary experience or education. Sixteen others were screened out before the oral examination. The final choice of the remaining candidates was Richard A. McGee, then the Supervisor of Public Institutions of the State of Washington. He was not a Californian and had no local political ties or obligations. But he was highly regarded by penologists as an effective administrator.

McGee had entered correctional work after experience in the field of higher education. From 1926 to 1930 he was an Instructor at the University of Minnesota. He left this post to become Supervisor of Education at the Federal Penitentiary, Leavenworth, Kansas in 1931, just at the beginning of the reform era in the Federal Bureau of Prisons. Two years later, he was transferred to the Federal Penitentiary at Lewisburg, Pennsylvania. Later he became Warden of the New York City Penitentiary at Riker's Island, Deputy Commissioner of Corrections of New York City, and Supervisor of Public Institutions of the State of Washington. He was elected President of the American Prison Association in 1943. His penal philosophy, career pattern, and experience epitomized correctional reform ideals.[1]

McGee was well versed in correctional history and theory. He became known for his ability to counteract the widespread tendency in prisons to substitute symbolic for substantive reforms. This change oriented approach in Washington State, from which he moved to California, was epitomized by this story which he told:

> I shall always remember my first visit to the State Prison at Walla Walla, Washington, in December 1941. I asked the warden for a list of his personnel. We went over them one by one, and he told me what each of them did. We came to one name with the title "Librarian." Upon inquiry, it developed that the "Librarian" was really the mail censor. When we came to

---

[1]A detailed statement of his management views, made while he was warden of the Riker's Island Penitentiary, included a proposal for centralized administration to guarantee minimum standards, employment of qualified personnel, and regard for the civil rights and personal requirements of prisoners. See Richard Allen McGee, "The Care and Treatment of the Untried Prisoner," *Proceedings, Sixty-seventh Annual Congress of the American Prison Association,* New York, 1938. See also his presidential address, "Correctional Administration in a Changing World," *Proceedings, Seventy-fourth Annual Congress of the American Prison Association,* New York, 1943.

the Chief Medical Officer, I asked what hours he worked. It developed that he came in daily at 7 in the morning and left one hour later. During the rest of the time the hospital was manned entirely by inmates, and the convict boss had the key on the inside. In another institution, right outside the warden's office, was a door with the words "Classification Department" printed in gold letters 3 inches high. I opened the door and looked in—and what did I see? A cubby hole six feet square, a desk and a chair, and at the desk was a chaplain with his feet on the desk and sound asleep.[1]

McGee assumed his new post with awareness of the task which confronted him: the reorganization of an administratively loose assembly of institutions into a coordinated department capable of applying correctional knowledge and ready to experiment to discover techniques superior to those that were traditional, but ineffective. He was not responsible for any of the policies of the past. He was a new man, selected after one of the most careful screening procedures ever used to select a public official. The State of California also had just passed legislation providing an administrative and legal framework that remedied many of the organizational inefficiencies which had plagued earlier prison administrators in California. McGee was assured strong executive support, free from political interference. He has been retained by two succeeding Governors: the Republican, Goodwin Knight (1952-1958), and the Democrat who succeeded him, Edmund G. Brown.

What happened in California was not merely of local concern. It was an undertaking of national interest from some of the country's most outstanding penologists who had a personal stake in helping this effort to succeed. For instance, James V. Bennett served as an occasional consultant, bringing the prestige of his office and experience to support the changes in progress in California. Austin H. MacCormick, a former chief of McGee, was the Executive Director of the Osborne Association, which is dedicated to penal reform and research. He soon was to become Professor of Criminology at the University of California at Berkeley, where he devoted a good

---

[1]Richard A. McGee: "Prisons at the Crossroads," *Proceedings of the Eighty-third Annual Congress of Corrections of the American Prison Association.* New York, 1953.

deal of his time and energy as a consultant on California's correctional problems.

RECRUITMENT OF A STRONG LEADERSHIP CADRE

When McGee took office, each of the State's prisons was under new leadership. The warden of Folsom resigned and was replaced by Governor Warren with Robert A. Heinze, a career parole officer. Governor Olson's appointees, Clinton T. Duffy of San Quentin and Kenyon J. Scudder of Chino, were retained, as was Alma Holzschuh, the Superintendent of the California Institution for Women. Abusive practices and corruption had been largely eliminated. New ideas of humane custodial care were being tried.

The Department of Corrections became centralized administratively with less autonomy in policy formation for the wardens and superintendents. A cadre of staff specialists in education, treatment, management, and personnel were assembled at the Department's headquarters to help each prison to modernize its operations. McGee added or promoted four of the persons who had competed with him in the Civil Service examination for the post of the Director of Corrections. He was not afraid of autonomous and able men. He sought them out.

The central office staff assumed final responsibility for budgeting, personnel policies, and the expansion of treatment services. Planning for future developments, public relations, and liaison with the Legislature and the Governor's office were also centralized. The Director of the Department meets several times each year with his superintendents and wardens and (usually separately) with the Associate Superintendents and Associate Wardens. Major departmental innovations are discussed by this group before they are made applicable to all institutions.

The objective of these meetings is to coordinate broad policies. But day-to-day management of staff and inmates remains a local responsibility. Tight centralization that would stifle all local initiative has thus been avoided. As a result, there developed many differences in institutional traditions, management policies, characteristics of inmates, and other factors. They were reflected in variations in the attitudes of personnel on many policy issues.[1] For instance, the superintendents of Tehachapi and Los Padres strongly encouraged their correctional officers—sergeants, lieutenants, and captains—to become group treatment leaders. At Tracy, top level administrators were favorably inclined to the idea, but only 10 per cent of the staff were active as counselors in 1959. At Vacaville, group counseling by custodial employees was not authorized until that same year (see Chart 3). These variations in management policies were viewed as "experiments" in administration, often care-

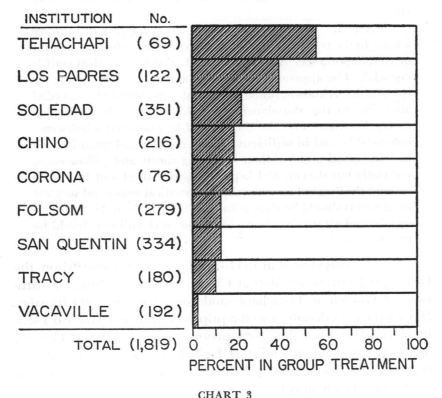

CHART 3

CURRENT PARTICIPATION OF CORRECTIONAL OFFICERS AND ADMINISTRATORS IN GROUP TREATMENT PROGRAMS

[1] A detailed analysis of our questionnaire data by institutions has been made by Kenneth Polk in *Custody, Punishment, or Treatment? A Study of the Attitudes and Behavior of Prison Personnel* (unpublished Ph.D. dissertation, University of California, Los Angeles, 1961).

fully studied by central office staff members before the formulation of over-all Departmental policies.

PLANT EXPANSION

XXX. Prison architecture is a matter of grave importance. Prisons of every class should be substantial structures, affording gratification by their design and material to a pure taste, but not costly or highly ornate. We are of the opinion that those of moderate size are best, as regards both industrial and reformatory ends.

XXXIII. A right application of the principles of sanitary science in the construction and arrangement of prisons is a point of vital importance. A competent and adequate medical staff is essential. The apparatus for heating and ventilating should be the best that is known; sunlight, air and water should be afforded according to the abundance with which nature has provided them; the rations and clothing should be plain but wholesome, comfortable, and in sufficient but not exaggerated quantity; the bedsteads, bed and bedding, including sheets and pillow cases, not costly but decent, and kept clean, well aired and free from vermin; the hospital accommodations, medical stores and surgical instruments should be all that humanity requires and science can supply; and all needed means for personal cleanliness should be without stint.[1]

Four prisons existed in 1944—San Quentin, Folsom Prison, the California Institute for Men at Chino, and the California Institution for Women at Tehachapi—and housed about 7,000 inmates. During the next decade, a well-equipped California Medical Facility was built at Vacaville. New prisons were also built at Corona, Tracy, and Soledad, and military facilities converted at Los Padres near San Luis Obispo, along with new forestry and work camps for minimum custody inmates.

The shortage of prison facilities, incidental to the depression and war years, was partly mitigated, although the plant expansion did not keep up with the growth of the inmate population. It exceeded 23,000 in 1961, making necessary a doubling up of inmates

---

[1]American Prison Association: "Declaration of Principles," *Proceedings of the 60th Annual Congress, 1930, op. cit.*

in many cells. Further increases in the number of offenders can be expected as California's general population increases. San Quentin prison, with a rated capacity of 2,821 inmates, was ordered to prepare to house 5,000. The California Institution for Men will have to accept 1,573 in space built to accommodate 872.[1] Somewhat less overcrowding will be necessary in other institutions.

This population pressure makes it more difficult to provide educational and treatment programs for all inmates. The overcrowding would even be more extreme if it were not for active efforts to release on parole all prisoners who can be trusted and whose record is such as to warrant this privilege. If penal policies were to require that all offenders be kept behind bars for the entire length of their prison sentences, a vast additional building program would have to be planned for the future. This fact lent added urgency to the development of reformation programs.

Along with expansion of prison facilities went improvements in physical care, food, and clothing.[2] The net per capita cost of each prisoner rose by 36 per cent between 1944 and 1960 (see Chart 8, page 186). Many administrative precautions were taken to prevent abuses, including regular inspections of sanitary conditions. While living accommodations fall short of what the inmates would like, a questionnaire survey of former inmates in 1958 indicated that about half of the willing respondents thought that feeding, clothing, and housing were excellent, 13 per cent thought that they were the poorest part of the program, and 38 per cent expressed no opinion on the subject.[3]

Plant expansion and the maintenance of decent standards for housing, clothing and feeding are never a complete recipe for penal reform. For every proposed physical improvement the question can be raised: "How can optimum social control be obtained?

---

[1] *The Correctional Review*, Vol. XVI, No. 4, June 14, 1961.

[2] The actual per capita cost in 1944 was 751 dollars and 1722 dollars in 1960. A standardization of these non-comparable dollar values by the Consumer Price Index in terms of 1947-49 dollars results in net per capita cost index of 999 dollars in 1944 and 1361 dollars in 1960.

[3] A survey of 238 inmates (40% of those contacted) made by a Special Study Commission on Correctional Facilities. The findings are reported by Winslow Rouse, *The Treatment of Offenders in the Prisons of California*, Sacramento, Board of Corrections, 1959, typed manuscript.

Through more program or more cement?" The issue has generally been resolved by compromise. The Legislature financed increases in inmate "warehousing" facilities, but to keep costs down, it also encouraged intra-institutional educational and treatment programs and early release on parole of eligible inmates. For instance, a Special Intensive Parole Unit, requiring the hiring of additional parole officers to provide more intensive supervision, was financed by releasing a sample of men three months before their normal parole dates. The money not needed to care for them in prison was used to pay for the new parole officers.

APPOINTMENT OF A TREATMENT PROGRAM PLANNER

III. The progressive classification of prisoners, based on study of the individual, and administered on some well-adjusted system should be established in all prisons above the common jail.

IV. Since hope is a more potent agent than fear, it should be made an ever-present force in the hands of prisoners, by a well-devised and skillfully applied system of rewards for good conduct, industry and attention to learning. Rewards, more than punishment, are essential to every good prison system.

V. The prisoner's destiny should be placed, measurably in his own hands; he must be put into circumstances where he will be able, through his own exertions, to continually better his own condition. A regulated self-interest must be brought into play, and made constantly operative.[1]

One of Director McGee's first acts in office was to induce Norman Fenton, the former head of the California Bureau of Juvenile Research, to take leave of absence from his post as Professor of Education at Stanford University. Fenton was a clinical psychologist with many ideas for introducing a comprehensive treatment program for inmates. His first assignment was to set up a Reception-Guidance Center at San Quentin Prison. All incoming prisoners were sent there for diagnosis and classification. Reports were written to provide a basis of rationalizing their assignment to the

---

[1]American Prison Association: "Declaration of Principles," *Proceedings of the 60th Annual Congress,* 1930.

variable custodial work, and educational sub-units of the prison system.

Fenton never returned to his university position. He became part of the Department's reform "brain trust." While he enjoyed teaching, and over the years conducted many training sessions for Departmental personnel, he has felt challenged by the opportunity to add a therapeutic dimension to the prison system by well considered administrative planning. He believes that clinical training was an important qualification for doing therapy, but that therapeutic attitudes can be fostered in any motivated employee. Fenton has worked patiently to encourage and teach personnel at every level of responsibility—whether they are wardens or guards—to expand the horizon of their work to include a concern for the rehabilitation of inmates.

Group treatment was among the rehabilitative techniques of prisoners discussed when Fenton was hired. A decade was to pass before group counseling became an identifiable and separate program in the Department of Corrections in the 1950's. At first, priority was given to expansion of existing reform activities. More ministers with special interests and qualifications for work with prisoners were being recruited, as were more and better qualified vocational and academic teachers, librarians, and recreation leaders. Fenton became heavily involved with administrative responsibilities for these programs, when in 1946 he moved from San Quentin to Sacramento as Deputy Director for Classification and Treatment.

The ultimate development of treatment programs in the Department of Correction has been greatly aided by the availability of these professionals. Ministers for many years had been the only category of prison employees strongly committed to a reform point of view, an expression of their concern for religious virtue, forgiveness, and charity. They hoped to inspire and convert inmates to goodness. In the early twentieth century, more and more of the prison reform leadership came from among educators. They were more secular in outlook, more convinced that men needed to be re-educated than converted. In the 1930's and 1940's, educators generally became increasingly influenced by psychological and psychiatric doctrines, which stressed the functions of therapy for remotivation. For instance, as early as 1944, some of the teachers at San Quentin incorporated group counseling in their curriculum. They did not hold their classes to a specific lesson plan if they thought it was more important for inmates to spend class-time talking about personal problems.

In 1954, after a comprehensive reorganization of the Department of Corrections, an organizational climate was produced, conducive to the rapid growth of a group treatment program. Library and teaching activities had been expanded in all institutions. Treatment personnel, including psychologists, psychiatrists, social workers, vocational counselors, and correctional counselors, had increased in number. In 1959, of the 3,654 employees answering our questionnaire, 159 were engaged in rendering welfare, mental hygiene, and other psychosocial treatment services. There also were 227 educators, 15 researchers, 48 physicians and dentists, 260 technicians, and 22 chaplains. In addition, 9 of the Department's policy makers were social workers, 5 were psychiatrists, and 2 each were respectively psychologists and sociologists.

These reform-oriented specialists had gained much influence throughout the Department of Corrections. Many had moved into policy making posts. And those promoted to policy positions from custody jobs did so often after getting advanced training or experience in education, sociology, psychology, and related mental health subjects. They helped to create an organizational atmosphere conducive to the rapid growth of an extensive group treatment program to be described in the next chapter.

PROFESSIONALIZATION OF STAFF

VII. Special training, as well as high qualities of head and heart, is required to make a good prison or reformatory officer. Then only will the administration of public punishment become scientific, uniform and successful, when it is raised to the dignity of a profession, and men are specially trained for it, as they are for other pursuits. The development of schools for the training of prison executives and guards, along the lines already started in this and other countries, should be promoted throughout the United States.[1]

The field of correction needs unusually well qualified staff members because they have extremely difficult assignments. Many deviants end in a state prison *after* other treatment and control agencies in the community have tried, but failed to deal with them. They can be described as "hard-core" cases, with few inner and environmental resources to support efforts at their rehabilitation. Few of them make a good living. Of the 12,512 inmates admitted between 1945 and 1949, 19 per cent were dull normal; 9 per cent had borderline intelligence; 4 per cent were mentally defective. About 12 per cent were illiterate.[2]

The proportion of mentally defective and illiterate inmates had dropped by 1960, but the prison population was still predominantly unskilled. It was less well educated than the general population.[3]

The caliber of employees of an organization is decisive for its effectiveness. Of special importance for the general organizational triumph of the reform point of view in California was the availability of the previously mentioned cadre of young men who had been hired in 1940 to staff the California Institution for Men. They had been trained from the start to rely on progressive principles of prison management, to be firm in setting limits, but humane in determining the means of setting them. Chino's in-service training course had included instruction in the use of firearms to reduce the chance of accidents. But after that, reports Mr. Scudder:

" . . . we locked up the guns, and they have never been used except in case of escapes. Through the use of judo, the art of self-defense, we developed in each man poise, courage, and confidence in his own ability to deal with any emergency that might arise without resorting to arms. A part of each day was

[1]American Prison Association: "Declaration of Principles," *Proceedings of the 60th Annual Congress*, 1930.

[2]Ronald H. Beattie: *California Prisoners, 1945-1949; An Analysis of Admission to and Release from California Prisons*. Sacramento, California, The Research Committee of the Board of Corrections, July 1, 1951.

[3]Winslow Rouse: *The Problem of Adult Correction: A Case Study of State Penal Administration in California*. Claremont, California. A dissertation presented to the general faculty of the Claremont Graduate School, 1961.

devoted to the theory of handling men and some sociology, psychology and the general philosophy of freedom that was to govern the institution."[1]

Thirty-nine of these men were still with the Department of Corrections in 1952. Five were Associate Wardens or Superintendents; five others were policy makers and on the Director's staff in Sacramento. Most of the others had been promoted to important positions. Together with a smaller number of treatment oriented persons recruited to staff the Reception-Guidance clinics, they provided the new Director with a core of professionals available to help him transform the rapidly expanding prison system into one that integrated humanitarian with control objectives.

COOPTATION OF CUSTODIAL EMPLOYEES TO SUPPORT REFORM GOALS

Assurance of safe custody had been the principal duty of correctional employees. Under McGee, education and treatment were given equal emphasis, in the spirit of one of the cardinal principles of the correctional movement:

II. The treatment of criminals by society is for the protection of society. But since such treatment is directed to the criminal rather than his crime, its great object should be his moral regeneration. Hence the supreme aim of prison discipline is the reformation of the criminal, not the infliction of vindictive suffering.[2]

This reform orientation was translated administratively by the appointment of two principal assistants to every prison warden: an Associate Warden-*Custody* and an Associate Warden-*Classification and Treatment*. Educational prerequisites were more important for the latter posts, but they were not irrelevant to the former. At the beginning, custody and education and treatment were Departmental interest groups differing considerably in their outlook. Departmental policy encouraged employees to study in their spare

---

[1]Kenyon J. Scudder: "Open Institution," *The Annals of the American Academy of Political and Social Sciences*, Vol. 293, May, 1954.

[2]American Prison Association: "Declaration of Principles," op. cit. *Proceedings of the 60th Annual Congress*, 1930.

time. By 1960, there was a high proportion of persons with educational qualifications among the Department's custodial personnel. Training differentials between custody, education, and treatment employees were becoming less marked. Mental health, education, and policy making personnel were still something of an educational "elite," but in all occupational categories there were persons with graduate education. They had the general background for promotion to posts that would give them responsibility for integrating the Department's manifold responsibilities to insure custody and encourage inmate education and treatment.

TABLE 5

EDUCATIONAL BACKGROUND OF MENTAL HEALTH PERSONNEL, POLICY MAKERS, EDUCATORS, AND CUSTODY ADMINISTRATORS, CALIFORNIA DEPARTMENT OF CORRECTIONS

(In Per Cent)

	Mental Health Personnel (N = 159)	Educators (N = 227)	Policy Makers (N = 98)	Custody Administrators (N = 350)
Junior high school—completed 7th through 9th grade	---	*	1	5
Partial high school—completed 10th or 11th grade but did not graduate	1	3	2	11
High school graduate	4	11	6	38
Partial college training—attended at least one year but did not graduate	9	18	22	41
Received college degree at Bachelor's level or equivalent (for example, teaching credential)	9	12	10	3
Academic work beyond Bachelor level or equivalent but not sufficient to obtain either a Master's or Doctor's degree	31	25	27	1
Master's level degree or degrees	34	30	21	---
Doctoral degree or degrees	11	1	10	---
Unknown	1	---	1	1
Total	100	100	100	100

*One educator reported to have had less than seven years of grade school education.

Among custody administrators (captains, lieutenants, and sergeants), correctional administration (13 per cent), sociology (6 per cent), and business administration (4 per cent) were preferred as areas of concentration for higher education. But one out of twenty had studied psychology, social work, or psychiatry. Somewhat more than half (54 per cent) never attended a University. This was true of only 9 per cent of the policy makers. The most common areas of their specialization were social work (13 per cent), business administration (11 per cent), and public administration (10 per cent), education, sociology, psychiatry and psychology were also well represented. Mental health personnel were most often trained in social work (22 per cent), psychology (19 per cent), and sociology (14 per cent). Education and vocational training predominated as educational background of the educators (76 per cent).

TABLE 6

EDUCATIONAL SPECIALIZATION OF MENTAL HEALTH PERSONNEL, POLICY MAKERS,
EDUCATORS AND CUSTODY ADMINISTRATORS, CALIFORNIA DEPARTMENT OF CORRECTIONS

(In Per Cent)

	Mental Health Personnel (N = 159)	Policy Makers (N = 98)	Educators (N = 227)	Custody Administrators (N = 350)
General high school	4	6	6	42
Special vocational training	2	6	37	13
General (Liberal Arts) college work	4	8	8	7
Social Work or Social Welfare	22	13	*	1
Psychology	19	6	4	4
Sociology	14	8	3	6
Education	4	9	39	1
Public administration	2	10	0	1
Correctional administration	9	3	*	13
Business administration	3	11	1	4
Psychiatry	8	8	0	1
Other	8	10	1	6
Unknown	1	2	1	1
Total	100	100	100	100

Before 1944, persons with special training and skills could rarely be induced to make a career in prison work, even at higher levels of responsibility. In 1959, even such low echelon jobs as correctional officers required a tenth grade education or its equivalent and four years of paid work experience. Plans are afoot to make high school graduation a minimum requirement. Nearly a third of the correctional officers have gone beyond high school to take college courses. For the Department as a whole, nearly half the employees have been to college. More than one in five is a college graduate. Two per cent have doctor's degrees (see Chart 4).

In correction, unlike the social welfare or the mental health departments, no academic field can claim a preferred professional jurisdiction over positions of administrative leadership or treatment. There are no clear-cut academic prerequisites for doing psychosocial treatment in prisons as there are in mental hygiene, school, or social work agencies. Social workers have become Wardens and Chiefs of Classification and Treatment. Sociologists have

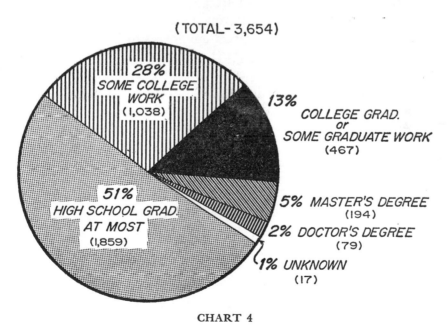

(TOTAL- 3,654)

28% SOME COLLEGE WORK (1,038)

13% COLLEGE GRAD. or SOME GRADUATE WORK (467)

51% HIGH SCHOOL GRAD. AT MOST (1,859)

5% MASTER'S DEGREE (194)

2% DOCTOR'S DEGREE (79)

1% UNKNOWN (17)

CHART 4

EDUCATIONAL BACKGROUND OF DEPARTMENTAL EMPLOYEES
(In Per Cent)

functioned as superintendents, group therapists, or consultants on milieu therapy. Several graduates in Public Administration are doing clinical treatment. Half of the people in mental health posts have had clinical academic training in social work, psychology and psychiatry, but treatment roles have also been assigned to sociologists (14 per cent), correctional administrator trainees (9 per cent), education majors (4 per cent), and others. There also are 14 per cent who had not graduated from college.

Prisons, like mental hospitals, are total institutions with an hierarchy of authority that is generally related to educational qualifications. But in prisons, there are few absolute barriers to mobility for lower echelon personnel. Correctional officers can conceivably become wardens, while attendants in mental hospitals cannot realistically expect to reach the comparable post of Hospital Superintendent.

Education is an advantage to employees. It enhances their chances of passing Civil Service examinations for a higher post. This fact may help to explain why large numbers of correctional employees mentioned plans for continuing their education. The Department of Corrections expects employees to know what they are doing and why they are doing it. Persons who want to be promoted know that they must be conversant with subject matter relevant, but not directly related to their jobs in order to pass written examinations.

We have no precise data on educational levels of employees in the Department of Corrections in 1944. It was generally low. By 1959, the Department's staff included a majority of persons who expressed interest in intellectual development. Higher education was a prized goal. The proportion of those who had plans for higher education was greatest among educators, researchers, parole officers, and mental health specialists. But there also were 15 per cent of the custodial administrators, 11 per cent of the technicians, 10 per cent of the correctional officers and supervisors of females who were actively studying to earn a higher degree (see Table 11).

It can only be surmised what influence is exerted on the Department by this education-oriented minority. New ideas are likely to be given attention by more than a few isolated intellectuals.

TABLE 7

PLANS FOR WORK TOWARD ADVANCED DEGREE BY OCCUPATIONAL CATEGORIES*

(In Per Cent)

Staff (N = 3,654)	No	Yes	No, But Plan to Take Some Courses in the Future	No Rresponse
Educators and Researchers (N = 242)	39	43	16	2
Parole Officers (N = 130)	49	25	24	2
Mental Health Professions (N = 159)	53	24	22	1
Supervisors of Females (N = 67)	55	10	33	2
Custodial Administrators (N = 350)	59	15	26	----
Correctional Officers (N = 1,470)	68	10	21	1
Technicians (N = 259)	72	11	16	1
Policy Makers (N = 98)	76	7	15	2
Maintenance Workers (N = 397)	79	4	15	2
Chaplains (N = 22)	82	5	5	8
Clerical and Office Workers (N = 413)	85	5	9	1
Physicians and Dentists (N = 47)	---	---	---	---
Total (N = 3,654)	68	13	19	—

*Response to question: "Are you currently working toward a college or university degree in an academic or professional area which you consider *relevant* to your career in the Department or Division?"

Certainly, these facts about educational plans do not lead one to suspect that the Department would have a *status quo* orientation.

In addition to extra-mural education, the Department has been conducting an active in-service training program, particularly for correctional officers and for group counseling leaders. A series of training manuals were written for these purposes. Half of all employees had some training as group leaders, a fact of special significance for the development of Department-wide treatment programs. The training course included reading of Norman Fenton's text on group counseling, which indicated to employees that treatment should be limited to persons who could answer "yes" to such questions as:

Are you tolerant?
Do you have genuine interest and respect for others as persons?

Are you broadminded towards people of minority groups?
Are you able to listen to criticism and fantastic questions from
   inmates without becoming angry?
Are you able to control yourself reasonably well, not to feel sorry
   for yourself even when you have worked hard and seem not to
   be appreciated by those whom you have tried to help?
Are you able to take advice?[1]

Ten per cent of the employees supplemented this in-service training with education in counseling at a university or institute. An
additional 4 per cent had training only at a university or institute.

IDENTIFICATION WITH THE FIELD OF CORRECTIONS

The professional identification of some, but not all categories
of employees, reflects their work milieu. This inference is derived
from data on membership in professional societies in the correctional field. The Department's social workers, sociologists, educators, public administrators, correctional administrators, and
business administrators were more often active in correctional
organizations than in societies in their own academic disciplines.
The reverse was true of psychiatrists and psychologists. They
showed a more frequent identification with their own disciplines
than with the correctional field (see Table 8).

Corrections in California is clearly on the road to professionalization. This development has been facilitated by the rapid expansion of prison facilities as the State as a whole was growing. There
were opportunities for promotions without having to fire or release
hold-overs from the old system. The penal system could advance
persons with ability to positions of increasing responsibility. In
1959, 32 per cent of the correctional officers had some college education. Technical knowledge and skill were expected from all employees, particularly in positions of responsibility.

Career Incentive 1: Job Security

When employees identify their own welfare with that of the
organization which employs them they bring more than energy to

---

[1]Norman Fenton: *An Introduction to Group Counselling in Correctional Service.*
Sacramento, California, Department of Corrections, 1957.

TABLE 8

<small>MEMBERSHIP IN PROFESSIONAL ORGANIZATIONS BY AREA OF ADVANCED EDUCATION,
DEPARTMENT OF CORRECTIONS*</small>

(In Per Cent)

	Correctional Organizations	Own Academic Fields	Other	None	Unknown
Social work or welfare, M.A. or above (N = 41)	66	36	10	15	——
Sociology, M.A. or above (N = 25)	44	20	44	16	4
Psychology, M.A. or above (N = 34)	41	50	23	18	——
Psychiatry, M.D. or Ph.D. (N = 21)	24	81	5	5	——

*Many employees reported belonging to more than one professional organization with the result that percentages exceed 100.

The majority of sociologists and psychologists had done work toward a Ph.D. but had not attained this academic degree. It is required for full-fledged status in their respective professional organizations. In social work the Master's degree is sufficient for full-fledged professional status.

their work. They are likely to take a long-range view of its problems and be motivated to perform near the optimum level of their potential. The Department offered employees incentive not previously enjoyed to any great extent: job security, rising pay scales, opportunity for promotion, and work in which to take pride.

Security was insured by placing all but a handful of correctional jobs under civil service. The newly appointed Director retained all employees, except for a part-time legal counsel whose function was abolished under the new legislation. Persons were fired only for gross incompetence. Once the merit system was instituted, fear of a capricious loss of employment ceased to be a means of enforcing conformity to organizational expectations. Between June 30, 1944, and June 30, 1960, the number of Departmental employees rose from 736 to 3790.1, a more than five fold increase. The expanding Department had many opportunities for both greater administrative responsibility and higher pay. Any system of secure tenure has among its consequences the retention of tired, disillusioned, ill, and unmotivated employees. But promotions

were made largely on the basis of competitive examination. They
are administered by the State Personnel Board to all eligible persons who want to take them.

Career Incentive 2: Pay Rises

We have no data on prison system salary levels in 1944. By
1959, the Department had a salary structure conducive to making
a career in prison work (see Table 9).

TABLE 9

MONTHLY SALARY, EMPLOYEES OF DEPARTMENT OF CORRECTIONS

(In Per Cent)

	Under $400	*$401-$500*	*$501-$600*	*$601+*	*Unknown*
Physicians and Dentists (N = 47)**	0	0	0	92	8
Policy Makers (N = 98)	1	1	14	83	1
Parole Officers (N = 130)	0	21	52	23	4
Mental Health Personnel (N = 159)	2	20	54	18	6
Technicians (N = 259)	31	39	16	12	2
Educators and Researchers (N = 242)	4	14	67	10	5
Chaplains (N = 22)	0	0	82	4	14
Custody Administrators (N = 350)	0	26	71	3	0
Maintenance Workers (N = 397)	7	41	49	3	*
Correctional Officers (N = 1,470)	34	64	1	0	1
Supervisors of Females (N = 67)	40	52	8	0	0
Clerical and Office Workers (N = 413)	82	17	0	0	1
Total (N = 3,654)	27	41	24	7	1

*Frequencies less than 1 per cent.

**Two per cent of the physicians and dentists stated their salaries as being
between $401-$500. The full-time rate of pay is much higher. They were coded
as unknown, since it was not determined what proportion of time they were reim-
bursed for.

Few people were being "raided" from the Department by salary inducements alone. For the Department as a whole, there was a progressive increase in real wages over the years. After making corrections for inflationary changes in the value of the dollar, the mean net increase in 1959 of income was just short of $100 per month for all persons first employed in the Department in 1954 (see Table 10).

TABLE 10

MEANS AND STANDARD DEVIATIONS OF NET MONTHLY SALARY INCREASE,
PERSONNEL OF THE CALIFORNIA DEPARTMET OF CORRECTIONS*

(In 1947-1949 Dollars)

Years Employed	Number of Employees	Mean Salary Increases	Standard Deviation**
0–1	629	$ 6	$ 16
2	406	30	31
3	260	65	39
4	397	87	40
5	194	100	37
6	260	117	51
7	150	138	63
8	200	140	61
9	88	148	66
10	181	164	83
11	165	172	83
12	122	162	76
13	77	166	99
14	54	183	114
15	38	191	114
16	37	195	112
17	28	257	165
18	34	265	172
19	12	165	83
20 and over	110	216	124
Unknown	212		
	N = 3,654		

*Standardized to correct for cost of living changes since the year of first employment in the Department.

**The standard deviation data indicate that two-thirds of any cohort of employees who had equal tenure received a mean salary plus or minus the number of dollars equal to one standard deviation. One-third of the employees were paid more or less than these middle-range amounts.

Length of employment is related to salary since each position has a number of nearly automatic annual increases. Larger than average increments, however, come with promotions and the upgrading of positions. The salaries of most policy makers, doctors, dentists, and parole officers rose with more than average rapidity. Few of them were among the slow gainers, those whose salaries advanced less rapidly than those of the average employee of equal length of tenure. In contrast, supervisors of female offenders, correctional officers, clerical and office workers were over-represented among persons whose pay advanced slowly (see Table 11).

TABLE 11

STANDARDIZED RATES OF SALARY INCREASE BY WORK FUNCTION*

(In Per Cent)

	Very Slow	Slow	Average	Fast	Very Fast	Unknown
Policy Makers (N = 98)	2	3	15	15	56	9
Physicians and Dentists (N = 47)	----	6	28	13	38	15
Parole Officers (N = 130)	4	2	29	21	35	9
Educators and Researchers (N = 242)	7	2	31	14	32	14
Mental Health Personnel (N = 159)	4	4	38	22	21	11
Chaplains (N = 22)	5	5	45	9	5	31
Maintenance Workers (N = 397)	8	8	50	17	11	6
Technicians (N = 259)	4	10	54	10	17	5
Custody Administrators (N = 350)	2	2	55	29	9	3
Clerical and Office Workers (N = 413)	12	12	61	8	4	3
Correctional Officers (N = 1,470)	4	12	74	4	1	5
Supervisors of Females (N = 67)	6	6	76	1	7	4
Total (N = 3,654)	6	9	58	11	11	5

*Comparison of each person's increase in salary since the date he was first hired to all others employed for an equal number of years.

The existence of differentials in salary improvement for persons of similar length of tenure suggests that the Department of Corrections does not rely on tenure alone to determine when individuals will be given a pay raise. Nothing short of a complete personnel study of the Department will fully explain what factors are related to promotion, but there is evidence that promotions are more rapid for employees who show interest in the Department's treatment point of view. Leaders in the Department's group treatment program were over-represented among those whose earnings rose relatively quickly. Thirty-five per cent of those currently doing group counseling had a fast rate of salary increase, as against only 15 per cent of those who never led a group and 31 per cent of those who once did, but no longer do group counseling (see Table 12). Counseling was at first a voluntary activity, often done on overtime without extra pay. People who can contribute to their jobs with enlightened self-interest, who have reserves of energy to do extra jobs and flexibility to try something new, are the kind who tend to get ahead in any organization.

Departmental employees were not quite so sure about the effect of participation in group counseling on promotion. Thirty-two per cent thought is was *true* that "staff people who volunteer to do group counseling with offenders improve their chances for promotion in the Department of Corrections." Forty-four per cent checked *uncertain*, but only 22 per cent thought this statement was false (see Table 2, page 55).

In general, the Department of Corrections was able to offer its employees more than a job. Its personnel policy encouraged them to think of a departmental career. Pay was at least equivalent to that of other branches of state government. Promotion was within reach of those who identified with the organization's objectives and were able to acquire the necessary technical qualifications.

Career Incentive 3: A Correctional Ideology

XV. In order to effect the reformation of imprisoned criminals, there must be not only a sincere desire and intention to that end but a serious conviction in the minds of the prison officers that they are capable of being reformed, since no man can heartily maintain a discipline at war with his inward beliefs; no

TABLE 12

PARTICIPATION IN GROUP TREATMENT PROGRAM BY STANDARDIZED SALARY INCREASE*

(In Per Cent)

Rate of Salary Rise	Never Led a Group (N = 2,367)	Current Psychotherapy (N = 64)	Current Counseling (N = 655)	Previous Psychotherapy (N = 24)	Previous Counseling (N = 511)	Unknown (N = 33)	Total in Per Cent
Slow (N = 517)	16	11	10	13	11	33	15
Average (N = 2,136)	63	34	49	21	53	55	58
Fast (N = 789)	15	42	35	59	31	6	22
Unknown (N = 212)	6	13	6	7	5	6	5
Total (N = 3,654)	100	100	100	100	100	100	100

*Difference between salary when first hired in the Department of Corrections and salary reported in January, 1959, adjusted for the following variables:

1. Changes in the value of the dollar.
2. Each person's net increment compared to the mean increase of persons who had been employed for the same number of years.

man can earnestly strive to accomplish what in his heart he despairs of accomplishing.[1]

Progressive ideals of prison management were vigorously espoused by the Department leadership. This policy was reflected in the fact it attracted many employees who shared these goals. They expressed attitudes that were indicative of pride in their work, a goal rather than an agency orientation, experimental venturesomeness, and a preference for reform over punishment objectives.

a. Pride in One's Work

In correction, as in other welfare services, the lack of recognition given to civil servants is a deterrent to recruitment and retention of qualified personnel. The economic rewards of work often seem to be more affected by the prestige of the customers than the skill required to perform it. Lawyers who help wealthy persons get a divorce are ranked and paid more highly than those who work for the Legal Aid Society. The legal work involved may be every bit as difficult. Psychiatrists in private practice rank professionally above those in State Mental Hospitals. Social workers in Child Guidance Clinics who have middle class neurotic parents and children as clients have more prestige than public assistance workers, who have many hard core cases in which neurotic problems are further complicated by poverty, poor health, and many types of social pathology. The complexity of the assignment of prison staff, responsible for the remaking of severely and chronically disturbed persons, stands in a similar contrast to the staff members' professional and public status.

The employees of the Department in 1959 were well aware of the modest status of their chosen field. They estimated that the public held their work in lower esteem than work with polio patients, mental patients, mental defectives, and people on relief. (See Chart 5.)

Policy makers, mental health employees, custody administrators, and research workers who have a relatively high identification with their jobs, ranked the prestige of their work low more often

[1]American Prison Association: "Declaration of Principles," *Proceedings of the 60th Annual Congress*, 1930.

MEAN RANK OF ESTIMATES BY DEPARTMENT OF CORRECTIONS EMPLOYEES OF HOW THE GENERAL PUBLIC EVALUATES THE RELATIVE WORTHWHILENESS OF HELPING SIX CATEGORIES OF CLIENTS

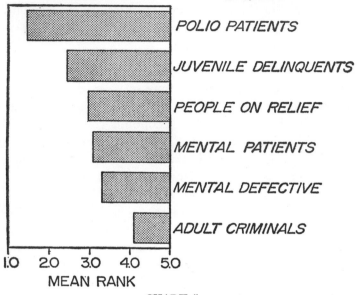

CHART 5

than did clerical, office, and maintenance workers, whose identification with corrections is less pronounced.

In spite of the low value accorded prison work by the public, Departmental employees expressed much personal interest in their field. More than half (56 per cent) of all Departmental employees said they wanted to stay in their jobs and/or in the correctional field, even if they inherited a sum of money upon which they could live comfortably without working. Seventeen per cent wanted to stop working; the proportion of leisure class aspirants was highest among clerical and office workers (33 per cent) and under 20 per cent for most other categories of workers. Only 9 per cent of the respondents stated a definite preference for employment outside the correctional field (see Table 13).

TABLE 13

PREFERENCE FOR REMAINING AT WORK EVEN IF NO EARNINGS WERE NEEDED*

(In Per Cent)

Staff	Stop Holding Regular Job	Keep Present Job	Change Employment to . . .		Can't Guess What I Would Do	No Response
			Better Job in Correctional Field	Outside Correctional Field		
Physicians and Dentists (N = 47)	6	50	10	9	21	4
Parole Officers (N = 130)	8	44	23	8	16	1
Chaplains (N = 22)	9	76	5	5	----	5
Policy Makers (N = 09)	10	54	15	4	14	3
Supervisors of Females (N = 67)	10	51	25	2	12	----
Mental Health (N = 159)	12	41	22	9	15	1
Educators (N = 227)	13	41	16	11	18	1
Correctional Officers (N = 1,470)	14	27	28	10	20	1
Maintenance (N = 397)	16	35	20	10	18	1
Technicians (N = 259)	17	42	16	9	15	1
Custody Administrators (N = 350)	20	33	25	7	14	1
Researchers (N = 15)	20	40	20	20	----	----
Clerical and Office (N = 413)	33	32	14	4	16	1
Total (N = 3,654)	17	34	22	9	17	1

*Response to question: "If, by chance, you inherited a sum of money such that you could live comfortably without working, what would you probably do about work?"

b. Goal Versus Agency Identification

A degree of interest in corrections as a professional "calling" rather than as a mere "job" can also be inferred from the frequency of critical responses towards *status quo* in the Department. Forty per cent of all employees disagreed; 19 per cent were neutral; and only 39 per cent agreed with the following statement:

> We can make some improvements in the Department, but, by and large, conditions in all institutions I know about are as good as they can be considering the type of prisoners that have to be kept there.

Critics were particularly numerous among mental health specialists (67 per cent) and policy makers (61 per cent). Expressions of support for the *status quo* were most common among correctional officers, technicians, maintenance, clerical, and office workers (see Chart 6).

Like every large bureaucracy, the Department of Corrections has a tendency to stress organization-mindedness. Many employees responded by adopting an "organization man" role,[1] but this was consciously counteracted by headquarter's encouragement of all employees to think about how to improve their jobs and express new ideas *within* the Department and its channels, even if critical of administrative practices. A pattern of rotating staffs of different prisons was introduced to integrate the Department and to make skilled persons from one institution (or from headquarters in Sacramento) available to others. Newsletters and informational memoranda were sent out frequently to keep lower echelon officials and staff informed of new ideas and proposals or to give explanations of why certain policies were being implemented. From time to time personnel development conferences were held in which top echelon officials met with middle range and lower echelon persons to discuss agency problems on an informal basis. These conferences were focused on the Department and its mission rather than on a particular prison or one of its sub-units.

---

[1] William H. Whyte: *The Organization Man.* New York, Simon and Schuster, 1956.

READINESS TO CRITICIZE STATUS QUO OF DEPARTMENT OF CORRECTIONS

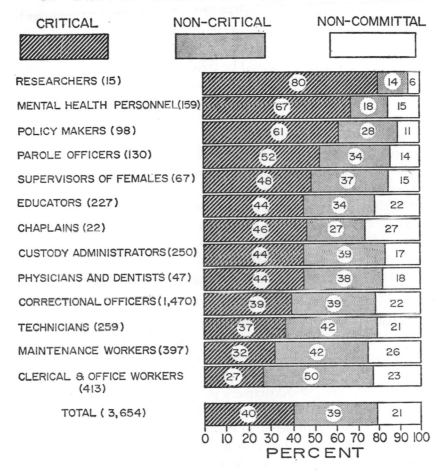

CHART 6

Response to question: "What do you think about the following statement?—We can make some improvements in the department, but by and large, conditions in all institutions I know about are as good as they can be, considering the type of prisoners that have to be kept there."

c. Experimental Venturesomeness

There is no conclusive evidence that educational, religious, and therapeutic activities in prisons facilitate the adjustment of inmates after they leave prison. The long-range rehabilitative impact of these programs is a matter of conjecture rather than proof. Nevertheless, in all categories of personnel there was at least a significant minority with optimism about the possibility that new techniques of treatment should be tried out. Policy makers, mental health specialists, chaplains, and educators were particularly likely to favor experimentation with new treatment programs even if it necessitated a lowering of security precautions. Correctional officers were more often emphatic on the primacy of taking few risks with custodial controls. Physicians, dentists, and technicians were intermediate in their outlook (see Chart 7). But in all categories of employees both of these viewpoints were represented. Six per cent of the custody administrators, who are directly responsible for the safekeeping and control of inmates, were willing to regard custodial considerations as secondary to setting up a new treatment program. Nine per cent of the mental health personnel expressed opposition to instituting a new program if security precautions would have to be lowered.

d. Reform Rather Than Punishment

The majority of the custody administrators (sergeants, lieutenants, and captains) were inclined to keep existing penalties or to increase them. Departmental policy makers, such as Associate Wardens, Wardens, headquarters personnel in Sacramento, along with mental health personnel, more often favored giving the Adult Authority greater latitude in granting paroles. Policy makers were also more often willing than custody administrators to house treated offenders in a hospital type of institution, either under Department of Corrections jurisdiction or outside of it, in the Department of Mental Hygiene. But no category of personnel, including custodial employees, was without many persons who expressed views in harmony with the treatment aims of the correctional reform movement (see Table 17, page 135).

OPINION ON EXPERIMENTATION WITH NEW TREATMENT PROGRAM
CALIFORNIA DEPARTMENT OF CORRECTIONS EMPLOYEES

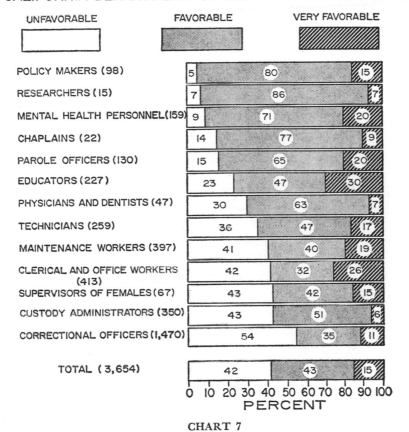

CHART 7

Percentages are based on the number of respondents in each category. Twenty-one, or slightly less than one per cent, did not answer this question. In no category of employees did the proportion of non-respondents exceed 4 per cent.

A "DUE PROCESS OF LAW" PRISON SOCIETY

XII. A system of prison discipline, to be truly reformatory, must gain the will of the prisoner. He is to be amended; but how is this possible with his mind in a state of hostility? No system can hope to succeed which does not secure this harmony of wills, so that the prisoner shall choose for himself what his officer chooses for him. But to this end, the officer must really choose the good of the prisoner, and the prisoner must remain in his choice long enough for virtue to become a habit. This consent of wills is an essential condition of reformation.[1]

Seasoned criminals often have considerable influence in the prisons in which they are incarcerated. We have no precise data on the role of confirmed criminal elements in California prisons in 1944. From descriptive evidence at hand and reports of observers, conditions were like those found by Clarence Schrag to exist in one unnamed western institution. He found inmate *leaders* did not differ from other prisoners in age, occupation, educational attainment, ethnic status, marital status, or intelligence test scores. They differed from ordinary inmates in being more anti-social.

Leaders rarely were first offenders or non-violent persons with short prison sentences. They served more time in prison, had longer sentences remaining to be served, were more frequently charged with crimes of violence, and were more likely to be repeated offenders. Significantly more leaders than other inmates were diagnosed as homosexual, psychoneurotic, or psychopathic. Finally, the institutional adjustment of leaders was marked by a significantly greater number of serious rule infractions, including escape, attempted escape, fighting, and assault.[2]

After 1944, inmate "trusties" in California prisons were eliminated from all but a few posts that had given them opportunities to exercise power. In 1960, a few inmates still exercised informal influence by virtue of being skilled tradesmen or clerks. But they were displaced from minor supervisory, teaching, and administrative posts by free personnel. This accounted in part for the reduction of the ratio of employees to inmates by about one-third between 1944 and 1960.[3] There also were many additions to the staff primarily concerned with the treatment of inmates. These addi-

---

[1] American Prison Association: "Declaration of Principles," *Proceedings of the 60th Annual Congress, 1930.*

[2] Clarence Schrag: "Leadership Among Prison Inmates," *American Sociological Review*, Vol. 19, February, 1954.

[3] The ratio of prisoners to staff on June 30, 1944 was 7.7. It dropped to 5.1 in 1956 and 5.3 in 1960.

tions greatly enhanced the capability of the officials to influence the prison milieu in support of socially acceptable goals. The group programs were one of the chief instruments by which staff members tried to reach both the hearts and minds of small groups of inmates, to motivate them to work on their reformation.

When many people interact in a large caste organization composed of free personnel and prisoners, they can work towards common objectives only to the extent that they share common goals and let one know what the other is doing. Communication is the life blood of every social system. Before 1944, mutual exchange of thoughts and feelings were opposed by the prison administration in California. An inmate who was seen talking informally to a correctional officer at either San Quentin or Folsom was risking censure from inmate "con" bosses, who were on their guard against "squealers." The employee might have to answer questions from his administrative supervisor about the reasons for such fraternization. He might even be suspected of taking a bribe. Each of the prisons was an almost closed world. But after 1944, communication channels, both formal and informal, were developed to enable the prison staff to influence the inmates and for the inmates to react to the staff.

Since 1941, the assignment of each inmate to an institution or camp within the prison system has been made in a Reception Guidance Center, after a detailed study of his background. Shortly after his arrival at the institution to which he has been assigned, he will be asked to appear in person before an Institutional Classification Committee. Chaired by the warden or superintendent, it includes top echelon administrators, a medical officer, a chaplain, an educator, and others. Throughout an inmate's stay in the prison, the Institutional Classification Committee reviews his prison program and adjustment. No prisoner is likely to become dependent on the whim of any one staff person for his treatment during the period of imprisonment.

Each prisoner is given a rule book detailing institutional regulations, inmate activities, duties, and privileges. When disciplinary violations occur, each employee is required to handle them in accordance with carefully worked out procedures. He cannot follow his whim of the moment.

For certain types of more serious violations, a formal charge against the inmate has to be filed. If the watch lieutenant of the area where the violation occurred feels it can be handled by a reprimand or counseling, the charge can be dropped. It can also be brought before a hearing officer, who has to hold a formal hearing in the presence of both the staff member charging a rule violation and the inmate who is alleged to have committed it. More serious charges will be heard by a "Disciplinary Committee," which includes both custody and treatment personnel. The offending inmate will be able to tell his side of the story before the Committee imposes one or more of the following punishments:

1. Reprimand.
2. Temporary or permanent loss of privileges.
3. One or more Sunday or holiday lock-ups.
4. Assignment to a special work detail.
5. Confinement in isolation cells for not more than thirty days.
6. Recommendation to the Adult Authority for appropriate action regarding redetermination of parole or discharge date.
7. Forfeiture of part or all of camp and correctional industry earnings.
8. Suspended sentence of action on any of the above punishments.[1]

Each punishment action must be reviewed by the warden or superintendent and formally noted in the inmate's file. The rule of law is carefully protected. No punishment can be imposed that would threaten an inmate's constitutional human rights or his health. Medical care is guaranteed to all.

The power of staff members, which once was nearly absolute, has to be exercised in a responsible manner. Inmates are provided with pay incentives for work in certain prison industries. Strict accounting procedures protect the outside income some of them receive in prison. Grievances can be expressed through newly

[1]Winslow Rouse: "The Problem of Adult Correction: A Case Study of State Penal Administration in California."

formed inmate councils or to individual officers through less formal channels.

Racial segregation practices have been largely, though not entirely, abolished. Equal cell and dining room accommodations are assigned to minority groups in the larger prisons where Negroes and Whites are sometimes kept apart. The Department has hired minority group staff members at every level of its operations. Our survey indicates that persons of Mexican origin, Negroes, and Jews progressed with equal or more than average speed, to the extent that salary increases can be used as an index of opportunity for advancement (see Table 14). This finding may, in part, be a consequence of the extra caution sometimes exercised by administrators when hiring minority group applicants. They have to be at least as well, if not better, qualified than average employees considered for comparable positions.

TABLE 14

PROGRESS OF MINORITY GROUP EMPLOYEES AS MEASURED BY STANDARDIZED SALARY INCREASES, DEPARTMENT OF CORRECTIONS**

(In Per Cent)

	Total Employees (N = 3,654)	Spanish-Speaking* (N = 101)	Negro (N = 73)	Yiddish-Speaking* (N = 30)
Slow and Very Slow	15	11	7	6
Average	58	67	71	47
Fast and Very Fast	22	20	21	34
Unknown	5	2	1	13

*Respondents to question: "What language other than English was most often spoken in your home?"

Only fifty persons called themselves "Mexican-American," as opposed to 101 whose parents often spoke Spanish. There were fifty-three persons who checked their religion as Jewish. For reasons related to machine processing requirements, data on salary increases were computed only for those thirty whose parents often spoke Yiddish.

**Difference between salary when first hired in the Department of Corrections and salary reported in January 1959, adjusted for the following variables: (1) Changes in the value of the dollar. (2) Each person's net increment compared to the mean increase of persons who had been employed for the same number of years.

One of the Reception-Guidance Centers is headed by a Nisei Associate Superintendent. The symbolic significance of this appointment, made on the basis of the usual competitive examination of all eligible candidates, is heightened by the recollection that only two decades earlier the State of California had laws that discriminated against persons of Japanese ancestry.

ENCOURAGEMENT OF INMATE-STAFF COMMUNICATION

XV. In prison administration, moral force should be relied upon, with as little admixture of physical force as possible, and organized persuasion be made to take the place of coercive restraint, the object being to make upright and industrious free men, rather than orderly and obedient prisoners. Brute force may make good prisoners; moral training alone will make good citizens. To the latter of these ends, the living soul must be won; to the former, only the inert and obedient body.[1]

Correctional officers have been instructed to get to know inmates as individuals rather than to fear that their action might be misinterpreted as "becoming too chummy." Inmate Advisory Councils were established in every prison. They can make suggestions, offer critiques of management policies, and ask direct questions of the prison's top manager, the warden or superintendent.[2] Group counseling, as will be shown later, was justified in part because it added still another communication channel between staff and inmates—one that affected lower levels of administration, not just top management.

Much has been done to encourage the maintenance of contact between inmates and the outside world. Visits from relatives and letter writing are made easier. Inmates are allowed to receive newspapers, hear radio and television programs, and print prison newspapers and have been given more freedom to talk to each other.

---

[1] American Prison Association: "Declaration of Principles," *Proceedings of the 60th Annual Congress, 1930.*

[2] Fred R. Dickson, Norman Fenton and Alma Holzschuh: "The Inmate Advisory Council," *Proceedings of the Eighty-fifth Annual Congress of Corrections of the American Correctional Association.* New York, 1955.

Libraries have been expanded and books have become easier to obtain.[1]

Improvements in communication was not intended to, nor has it resulted in the abolition of differences in status and outlook between the prison staff and the inmates. Those who can leave through the gate, and those who cannot, those who get paid for working in the prison, and those who are required to remain there by force, are separated by caste differences that are deeply rooted in law and custom. The administrative policy to free communication channels between the inmate and staff world did not have as its objective the breakdown of status differences which are inherent in the very concept of a total institution, especially a prison. Inequality in power is a necessary part of running a social system where men are incarcerated. But there has been a shift in how power is exercised: now there is more reliance on moral and therapeutic influence and less on the use of force. The consensus among our informants is that California prisons today harbor less fear and suspicion than used to be observable in the interaction between "cons" and their keepers. Without a study of the inmate culture it is not possible to know how the therapeutic prison idea has affected the inmates' sub-culture. But there is definite evidence in our attitude survey that it is reflected in the way employees perceive the prison in which they work. Only one in ten reported feeling that he was often faced with the potential of violence and escape.

The actual and symbolic importance of the gun and club as control devices has decreased markedly since 1944. Our survey showed that prison employees in all categories were quite willing to have casual and necessary social relations with inmates after their release on parole. But many also favored maintaining a degree of *social* distance between themselves and criminals. Only about half of the correctional officers and administrators were willing to employ released prisoners in their business or farm, something which 80 per cent of the mental health personnel and policy makers were willing to do.

---

[1]David Kantor: "The Real Value of a Library in a Correctional Institution and How to Achieve It," *Proceeedings of the Eighty-fourth Annual Congress of Corrections of the American Prison Association,* New York, 1954.

TABLE 15

Perception of Experience With Violence, California Department of Corrections Employees*

(In Per Cent)

	No Experience With Violence	Minor Experience With Violence	One or More Experiences of Serious Violence	Faced Often by Potential Violence and Escape	Unknown
Clerical and Office Workers (N = 413)	91	5	1	1	2
Physicians and Dentists (N = 47)	60	34	6	---	---
Technicians (N = 259)	47	27	17	7	2
Chaplains (N = 22)	41	36	9	9	5
Educators and Researchers (N = 242)	39	39	17	4	1
Maintenance Workers (N = 397)	30	43	21	5	1
Policy Makers (N = 98)	30	20	33	17	---
Mental Health Personnel (N = 159)	33	32	25	10	---
Parole Officers (N = 130)	17	48	28	6	1
Correctional Officers (N = 1,470)	15	39	34	10	2
Supervisors of Females (N = 67)	12	39	31	18	---
Custody Administrators (N = 350)	1	14	57	25	1
Total (N = 3,654)	30	32	28	10	---

*Response to question: "What has been your experience with inmates where there was the immediate and present danger of violence and escape?"

Willingness to communicate with inmates on the part of staff was not tantamount to social acceptance. Only a minority of employees in all categories expressed themselves as willing to have a parolee as a close friend, and even fewer would approve of his marrying into their family (see Table 16).

In 1960, the Superintendent of one of the larger prisons persuaded the Department to approve the hiring of an ex-prisoner as clerk in the accounting section, when he was discharged on parole. He does not go into the prison's security area. Free staff showed little concern regarding this innovation, but some of the prisoners were afraid that the employment of an ex-inmate would give the prison staff too much access to "secrets" of the inmate culture and informal social structure. The hiring of other carefully selected ex-inmates is under consideration. This is being done in part because it is illogical for the Department of Corrections to rule out

TABLE 16

STAFF ATTITUDES TOWARD PAROLEES*

(In Per Cent)

	Mental Health Personnel (N = 159)	Policy Makers (N = 98)	Custodial Administrators (N = 350)	Correctional Officers (N = 1,470)
Approve of a parolee marrying into your family	23	18	7	7
Have a parolee as a close intimate friend	41	29	12	13
Approve of having a parolee as a neighbor living next door	77	68	50	47
Have a parolee as an employee in your small business or farm	79	80	52	52
Approve a casual and necessary associations with parolees	87	86	88	77

*Response to question: "Assume that you are the proprietor of a small business or firm or a small farm and no longer actively working in corrections. How would you probably respond to 'the average' convict on parole?"

the occasional employment of an ex-convict, at the same time that officers appeal to other State Departments and private employers to employ parolees on jobs they can perform.

THE PRISON: A TREATMENT CENTER

Diagnostic Assignments. It will be recalled that the establishment of a diagnostic and classification center staffed by trained personnel was among the first actions of the new Director of Corrections. All new inmates are first sent to this center for individual study before administrators decide which of alternate prisons might be the most suitable for their treatment and reformation. Diagnoses of what inmates need were and are more clinically differentiated than the Department's facilities, but there was, in 1961, considerable variation as to what programming was feasible for inmates in different institutions. For instance:

1. California has a Medical Facility at Vacaville. It is a prison under medical direction, especially staffed to care for mentally ill, sexually deviant, tubercular, severely alcoholic and other special medical problem cases.

2. The California Men's Institution at Los Padres, San Luis Obispo County, is designed to house elderly inmates, many of them with chronic diseases, physical handicaps and dietary problems.

3. A special vocational training and educational center for youthful offenders is operated at Deuel in cooperation with the Department of the Youth Authority.

4. Most installations have some individual group treatment programs. One of them, the minimum custody prison at Tehachapi, requires that all inmates be involved in group counseling.

5. Work programs exist in all institutions, but all suffer from insufficient employment and a shortage of vocational training opportunities.

6. There are a variety of minimum custody facilities, including road and forestry camps.

7. There are several medium and maximum security facilities, including isolation units in several prisons for inmates who have an institutional record of assault, constant disciplinary infractions and aggressive homosexuality. These *Special Adjust-*

ment Centers are governed by strict rules to safeguard a treatment quite different from the primitive function that was characteristic of dungeons. In theory no restriction on any individual inmate is introduced without evidence of its necessity. Custodial staff for these isolation cells are selected to weed out sadistic and hostile personalities and to give authority, whenever possible, to persons with a treatment point of view. They are expected to ease the regime whenever possible, with the ultimate object of returning recalcitrant inmates to the general population of prisoners.[1]

The diagnostic staff of the Department knows these resources and what persons with special qualifications are working in different installations. It is, therefore, often possible to assign qualified personnel to work with a particular inmate, who has been diagnosed as being amenable to intensive psychosocial counseling or benefiting from a course in automobile repairing. The proportion of persons for whom this can be done is not the same in all institutions. But for the Department as a whole, state budgeting authorities allocated funds to expand various reform programs. They included academic education, industrial and shop training, religious services, libraries, inmate advisory councils, recreation programs, and experiments with intensive psychosocial treatment in prison and on parole.

Academic Education. The intelligence of prison inmates is not inferior to that of the general population. But the median level of academic accomplishment is only seventh grade as compared to an eleventh grade average for the adult population twenty-five years and over of the United States as a whole in 1959.[2]

Academic education was expanded by taking advantage of California's extensive adult education program, financed by state subsidies to local school boards. Since reimbursement is on the

---

[1]Allen Cook, Norman Fenton and Robert A. Heinze: "Methods of Handling the Severely Recalcitrant Inmate," *Proceedings of the Eighty-fifth Annual Congress of Corrections of the American Correctional Association*, New York, 1955. To what extent the custodial staff implements this policy is uncertain. The question was not covered by our survey.

[2]Winslow Rouse: "The Problem of Adult Corrections. A Case Study of State Penal Administration in California." Unpublished Ph.D. dissertation, Claremont Graduate School, Claremont, California, 1961.

basis of average attendance and prisoners can be depended upon to attend regularly except when ill, the Boards of Education have no budgetary problem to provide all the education which prison inmates can use. Graduating students receive a diploma which carries only the name of the local school district. No mention is made of the prison. The graduate, therefore, can use his grade school or high school certificate without having to be ashamed of it.

Free correspondence courses in college and technical subjects are available to qualified students. The only requirement for continuation is that the student maintain an acceptable level of scholarship. On completing college extension courses, students receive appropriate college credits from the University of California.

Industrial and Shop Training. The great majority of prison inmates are unskilled. This is particularly true of the younger men. Winslow Rouse reports that approximately 80 per cent of all male prisoners twenty-five years and under never acquired any usable or salable skill.[1] Youthful criminals were largely persons who were at a disadvantage in finding good jobs. Even among older age groups, with longer history of employment, the majority were unskilled. Crimes are probably not committed with equal frequency in all segments of the population. Certainly apprehension and conviction is more likely for offenders who are ignorant, unskilled and poor. The absence of useful employment in prison is also quite demoralizing.

In 1885 it was estimated that 75 per cent of the prison inmates in the United States were engaged in productive labor. By 1940, the total was reported to be much lower, 44 per cent for the country as a whole,[2] and 50 per cent in California.[3]

This reduction in work opportunities is related to several types of pressure. Industry labor groups are against competition from goods produced with cheap convict labor. Prison reformers object to the use of hard and often uneconomic work projects such as the Stone Quarry at Folsom Prison. They are more punitive than productive.

---

[1] *Ibid.*: 27-32.

[2] Richard F. Jones: "Prison Labor in the United States, 1940," *Monthly Labor Review,* Vol. XLIII, 1941.

[3] Austin MacCormick: Handbook of American Prisons and Reformatories, Vol. II, *Pacific Coast States.* New York, The Osborne Association, 1942.

The Department of Corrections has expanded its industry program to include textile production, furniture making, farming, forestry, fire fighting, road work, auto license plate making and others. Those employed can receive a small wage incentive of not more than ten cents an hour after a probationary period. Part of the income is retained, as a forced saving, to be available to the inmate at the time of his release. The remainder can be used to purchase canteen items or to help his dependents. In addition, somewhat more than 10 per cent of the prison population in 1955 was enrolled in full or part-time vocational training. Much of it was organized around prison maintenance activities such as baking, cooking, plumbing, and the like. A total of thirty-five trades are taught including auto mechanic work and carpentry.[1]

In order to gain the support of industry and labor for these efforts, an advisory Correctional Industries Commission was set up. It is chaired by the Director of Corrections, and included two labor representatives, two from industry, one from agriculture, and one representing the general public. In addition, labor-industry advisory councils of public spirited citizens are appointed for each of the major departmental institutions.

In addition to organized work programs, there are prison hobby shops to produce handmade craft items or paintings for sale to the general public through a store at each major prison. Inmates pay for their own materials and small tools. They can put their own price on the product and they receive all the income but 10 per cent of the income, which is added to the inmate welfare fund to help defray the cost of this program.

The industrial and shop training program is expensive. It requires extensive equipment and a staff of skilled supervisors. Ex-prisoners who acquired a trade skill in prison had 50 per cent fewer parole violations than those who had not received vocational training.[2] It is possible, however, that the kind of people who volunteer for training and who complete a course are also the type of persons who would in any case do well after leaving prison.

---

[1]Winslow Rouse: "The Problem of Adult Corrections: A Case Study of State Penal Administration in California."

[2]California Department of Corrections: *Report to the Governor's Council*, November 28, 1955.

Religious services are the oldest treatment service in prison. Before 1944, chaplains were the only well entrenched service with a reform orientation. In 1958 their range of service was extensive. Former inmates ranked religion as third important among prison treatment activities, although the majority of institutional chaplains told the staff of the Board of Correction Study Commission that their training was not being properly utilized in the total institutional program and that their duties tended to become routine.[1]

Libraries have been given funds to purchase books prisoners want to read rather than to depend largely on donated volumes. Trained librarians supervise inmate assistants in bookbinding, cataloging, and shelving books in accordance with good library standards. Librarians promote and sponsor music clubs, chess clubs, debating teams, Great Book Clubs, and similar inmate activities. By providing necessary reading material, the libraries greatly facilitate academic and vocational training. Prisoners who can read borrow from forty-five to over one hundred books a year, far more than the average borrower of a general community library.[2]

Inmate Advisory Councils have been organized. Members who are democratically elected are expected to conduct their business in accordance with a set of by-laws. They have no operational, disciplinary, or executive power, but the Executive Committee of the Inmate Advisory Council commonly meets with the warden or superintendent. While no personalities or problems of individual inmates can be taken up, the councils are free to discuss prison policies and request official information regarding them.

These Inmate Advisory Councils are viewed as being useful as a preparation for prisoners assuming democratic and social responsibility for the welfare of others.[3] It is not known to what extent they have this desired impact, but they certainly are useful in silencing false rumors that crop up among inmates in every total institution. The Councils have also helped to encourage inmate

---

1Winslow Rouse: "The Problem of Adult Corrections: A Case Study of State Penal Administration in California."

2*Ibid.*: 36. The statistics apply to the sample of persons studied by the Study Commission. No average volume of readership was reported in the Winslow Rouse study.

3*Ibid.*: 171-172.

participation in treatment programs and in philanthropic activities such as blood donating, Community Chest drives, and medical experimentation.

Recreation programs have been established, under the direction of civil service specialists, most of whom are college graduates, with a major in physical education. They conduct an active athletic program.

Many prisons also promote dramatic clubs, glee clubs, and a band. The Department furnishes instruments. There are headsets in every cell, where inmates may listen to one of two radio programs recommended by an inmate committee that is directed by the staff. At temporary institutions and camps, privately owned radios are permitted. In almost all of the prisons, inmates can own a record player and records. In the newer units, which have day-rooms attached to housing units, television sets are furnished. They are not available, however, in many units of the older institutions, San Quentin and Folsom, for lack of proper physical arrangements for viewing by large groups.[1]

Indeterminate Sentences. Modern penologists view prison reform as something more than the prevention of abuses in correctional institutions. They want positive action to substitute treatment for incarceration as the primary goal of imprisonment. This requires a legal framework which does not fit punishment to the crime, but to the criminal. In the words of the correctional movement's *Declaration of Principles:*

> VIII. Peremptory sentences ought to be replaced by those of indeterminate length. Sentences limited only by satisfactory proof of reformation should be substituted for those measured by mere lapse of time.[2]

California already had an indeterminate sentencing procedure when the Department of Corrections was organized in 1944. Lower and upper legal limits for the length of incarceration were set by law for different felonies. The actual length of time served within the limits was determined by the Adult Authority, a full-time

---

[1]Winslow Rouse: "The Problem of Adult Corrections: A Case Study of State Penal Administration in California."

[2]American Prison Association: "Declaration of Principles," *Proceedings of the 60th Annual Congress, 1930.*

parole board appointed by the Governor. It acted on the basis of information obtained from a study of each inmate and his behavior in prison and a hearing at which each inmate could tell his side of the case.

California makes extensive use of parole, which aims to test inmate capacity for self control and adjustment while he is still under sentence and can be returned to prison at the first sign of maladjustment. This theory is only imperfectly applied. The network of parole agents throughout the state is too small to accomplish more than supportive surveillance except for a minority of cases.

Parole officers do make preventive arrests if they see their charges in circumstances that violate conditions of parole, but they prefer to assume the role of counselor, employment agent, and social worker. In the 1950's, parole officers had lengthy discussions about whether they should carry guns. They now rarely do. The theory of parole has shifted from a primary concern with surveillance to treatment.

Experiments with Intensive Treatment. In 1953, the Legislature authorized the Adult Authority—the state parole board for men—to release selected inmates three months early on condition that they would receive intensive parole supervision in the community. While the average adult parole officer had about ninety parolees, officers of Special Intensive Parole Unit (SIPU) were assigned only fifteen. The hope was that the intensively counseled men would adjust better than those under routine parole supervision and that such a result would ultimately lead to a more intensive type of casework throughout the Division of Adult Paroles. Social workers and other clinically trained parole officers became influential in these SIPU units. A medically directed Out-Patient Clinic was set up in Los Angeles.[1] Higher education generally and social

[1]Walter T. Stone (for Ervis Lester): "New Concepts in Release Procedures," *Proceedings of the Eighty-third Annual Congress of Corrections of the American Prison Association,* New York, 1953; Walter T. Stone, "Administrative Aspects of the Special Intensive Parole Program," and Bernard Foreman, "Report on the Special Intensive Parole Unit-Research Investigation by the Division of Adult Paroles, Adult Authority, State of California," *Proceedings of the Eighty-sixth Annual Congress of Corrections of the American Correctional Association,* New York, 1956.

work, psychological, and psychiatric sophistication in particular were given recognition as qualifications for promotion in the Parole Division, although this trend was contested and sometimes counteracted by more custodially oriented officials.

The Special Intensive Parole Units have been continued and expanded although initial research findings have failed to show that intensively treated parolees adjust better than those under routine supervision. These same data, however, indicate that selected prisoners can be released three months early without added danger to public safety. Of 1,342 men whose parole dates were advanced, 14.7 per cent experienced a major arrest within six and one-half months, as contrasted with 15.3 per cent of 2,451 men released on the regular parole date. The money saved by releasing men from prison before their time was up more than paid for the added cost of their parole supervision.[1]

"Intensive" treatment units have also been established in several prisons. Therapists have worked with selected inmates individually once or more a week, and sometimes the same inmates have also received group treatment as well. The parole adjustment upon release from prison of these relatively intensively treated inmates has been compared to that of control groups of routinely treated inmates. Preliminary findings show no stable significant differences between the intensively and routinely treated inmates, but results, encouraging for the program, have emerged when inmates are diagnostically screened for their treatment potential.

Older adolescents who at admission to the Deuel Vocational Institution had been rated as being *amenable* to treatment and who received therapy, adjusted better on parole than three control groups: (1) Inmates rated as equally amenable who received no other than routine therapeutic attention; (2) inmates who had been rated as not being treatment amenable, but did receive therapy; (3) non-amenable rated prisoners who received only routine care.[2]

---

[1] Ernest Reimer and Martin Warren: "Special Intensive Parole Unit," *National Probation and Parole Association Journal*, Vol. 3, No. 3, July, 1957.

[2] Stuart Adams: "Interaction Between Individual Interview Therapy and Treatment Amenability in Older Youth Authority Wards," Board of Corrections, Monograph No. 2, *Inquiries Concerning Kinds of Treatment for Kinds of Delinquents*, Sacramento, California, July, 1961.

In general, departmental strategy has been to pursue a counseling program for a specified period of time, while data are collected to test the program's relevance to staff ratings of prisoner adjustment, parole violations and return to prisons from parole. If the findings fail to show a significant difference in favor of the treatment group, changes have been made in treatment procedures and techniques for selecting inmates for this special attention. The point of view expressed in this strategy can be summed up as follows: Prisons get a diverse population of problem cases. No single pattern but many variations of treatment programs are needed. And some of the inmates may be untreatable by means currently known. No one can expect to find a single treatment panacea. But he can search for combinations of treatment procedures that will have a favorable impact on certain categories of inmates even if they fail to help others.

While the range and extent of these services are far below the professional standards administrators would like to attain, the Department of Corrections has succeeded between 1944 and 1961 in setting up a structure in which access to such services becomes routine. The shortcomings of the programs were subjected to Departmentally initiated study and clearly recognized. They were called repeatedly to the attention of the Governor and legislative committees.

These developments carry out several of the recommendations of the *Declaration of Principles:*

> IX. Of all reformatory agencies, religion is first in importance because most potent in its áction upon the human heart and life.
>
> X. Education is a vital force in the reformation of fallen men and women. Its tendency is to quicken the intellect, inspire self-respect, excite to higher aims and afford a healthful substitute for low and vicious amusements. Recreation is considered to be an essential part of education. It has come to be recognized that recreation is an indispensable factor of normal human life. This principle is now heartily endorsed by prison administrators. Education in its broadest sense is, therefore, a matter of primary importance in prisons.
>
> XVI. Industrial training should have both a higher devel-

opment and a greater breadth than has heretofore been, or is now commonly given to it in prisons. Work is no less an auxiliary to virtue than it is a means of support. Steady, active, honorable labor, with reasonable compensation to the prisoner, is the basis of all reformatory discipline. It not only aids reformation, but is essential to it. It was a maxim with Howard, "make men diligent, and they will be honest"—a maxim which this congress regards as eminently sound and practical.

XXXIV. Probation and parole are among the most vital factors in the rehabilitation of the delinquent and the criminal. Probation is the release of the convicted delinquent under competent supervision, without commitment to an institution. Parole is a conditional release of the prisoner after having served a portion of his sentence. The overcrowding of our prisons, and the demoralization of young and inexperienced criminals by vicious association, can be greatly diminished by the use of these measures, but these two plans are ineffective unless efficiently organized with trained competent and well-paid probation and parole officers.[1]

TREATMENT ATTITUDES

The capability of a prison system to render treatment services depends on the concern of its staff for this function. One of the Department's objectives was to develop a high degree of acceptance of a therapeutic orientation among its employees. Our attitude survey disclosed that persons with a reform point of view were employed at every level of operation (see Table 17). In response to three nearly identically worded questions dealing with armed robbers, drug offenders, and homosexuals, custody administrators (sergeants, lieutenants, and captains) were more inclined, however, to keep existing penalties or to increase them than Departmental policy makers, such as Associate Wardens, Wardens, and headquarters personnel in Sacramento. The latter, as well as mental health personnel, favored giving the Adult Authority more latitude in granting paroles. They were also more favorably disposed to the suggestion that offenders be treated in hospital-type institutions,

---

[1]American Prison Association: "Declaration of Principles," *Proceedings of the 60th Annual Congress, 1930.*

either under Department of Corrections or Department of Mental Hygiene jurisdiction.

Differences in outlook between the more reform and more punishment oriented correction officials were a matter of degree rather than of mutually exclusive convictions. Proponents of both penal philosophies were agreed upon the ultimate objective of correctional work: the attainment of maximum social control over deviance. No society can survive if the laws and mores can be violated without constraints. Whereas reform oriented persons prefer to rely on *internal* constraint on prisoner self-control as much as possible, the more punitively oriented officials are pessimistic about the effectiveness of this approach. They believe maximum effectiveness can be expected when there is reliance on *external* controls, the threat of severe punishment, police surveillance, and strict law enforcement. Reform oriented persons, while recognizing that it is difficult to develop self-control in persons who have not in the past shown this capacity, are even more pessimistic regarding society's capacity for improving effective controls through surveillance. They favor the taking of risks by allowing inmates some leeway in prison and on parole to test their capacity for self-control as was shown in Chart 7, page 115: *Opinion on experimentation with new treatment program.*

When custody is an over-riding requirement, as it is with dangerous and mentally disturbed prisoners, there is no issue about maintenance of maximum surveillance. Such inmates are always locked up, carefully guarded, and not allowed to meet their visitors except through a glass partition. They get few opportunities to demonstrate their capacity for self control. But for the prison population as a whole, treatment oriented administrators believe they must take chances if the prison is to reform at least a portion of its population. In minimum custody prisons, forestry camps, and pre-release living units, prisoners are able to escape. They can abuse their freedoms in other ways as well. Treatment oriented persons argue that it is better to give them a chance to test their capacity to live up to social expectations while still under surveillance, than to wait until the completion of their sentences and their unconditional release. Then they can be apprehended only after new crimes are committed and proof of these can be obtained.

TABLE 17

COMPARISON OF REFORM AND PUNISHMENT RESPONSES OF CUSTODY ADMINISTRATORS, POLICY MAKERS AND MENTAL HEALTH PERSONNEL

(In Per Cent)

	Custody Administrators (N = 350)			Policy Makers (N = 98)			Mental Health Personnel (N = 159)		
	Reform	*Punishment*	*Unknown*	*Reform*	*Punishment*	*Unknown*	*Reform*	*Punishment*	*Unknown*
Recommendations for revision of homosexuality laws	74	21	5	91	5	4	91	9	—
Policy regarding opiate addicts	72	21	7	87	10	3	89	6	5
Policy regarding death penalty	35	61	4	81	14	5	80	15	5
Recommendations for revision of robbery laws	28	65	7	59	34	7	65	25	10

The respondents were given three nearly identically-worded questions, dealing with armed robbers, drug offenders and homosexuals. They were also asked a question on the death penalty. In each question they could check one of six responses as the one most closely describing their point of view. (See Questions CC, EE, KK and PP in Appendix B.)

Reform Responses:
1. Give Adult Authority complete latitude to parole, even without prison sentences in some cases.
2. Treat offenders as sick persons in a hospital-type institution in the Department of Corrections or in the Department of Mental Hygiene.
3. Abolish or restrict the use of the death penalty.

Punishment Responses:
1. Increase penalties.
2. Keep penalties pretty much as they are.

The exact distribution of reform and punishment attitudes among Department of Corrections personnel employed in 1944 is not known. But in the judgment of persons who have been with the Department since its inception, there has been a steady increase of relatively reform-oriented employees, with a proportional reduction of influence of custodial and punitively-oriented persons. The latter are losing influence, even among the generally more traditional administrators, security, and maintenance personnel. In every institution and all Departments there were in 1959, a cohort of custodial and other staff members personally identified with the hope that prisons could become effective instruments of rehabilitation. Most of them were not starry-eyed unrealists. They had an appreciation of the structural and ideological obstacles that impeded the attainment of correctional reform ideals.

EXPLORING THE UNKNOWN

XXIX. Uniform criminal statistics, gathered from every state, and skillfully digested, are essential to an exhibition of the true character and working of our correctional systems. The collection, collation and reduction to tabulated forms of such statistics can best be effected through the appropriate federal bureau.[1]

The management of uncertainty can serve as a good indicator of organizational commitment to the use of science in policy formulation. Administrators in the Department of Corrections have frequently acknowledged, informally and publicly, that there were many unresolved issues in prison management. Under the new regime, employees do not have to oversell an idea in order to get permission from Director McGee to experiment with it. Systematic efforts are expended to educate the public about the complexities of penal problems. Facts about prisons and prisoners, including those whose impact is discouraging, are reported periodically. When an inmate has escaped, newspapers have been informed immediately and reporters have been given the facts. Representatives of agricultural interests, of industrial and business management, as well as union officials were brought into the prisons to advise

[1]American Prison Association: "Declaration of Principles," *Proceedings of the 60th Annual Congress,* 1930.

on vocational work and prison industries and to give suggestions regarding educational and placement policies. Employees of the Department have been encouraged to participate as individuals in professional organizations related to their work.

Research has become a major organizational function. Much encouragement came from the Board of Corrections, established in 1944, to coordinate the state penal agencies for youths and for adults.[1] Among its functions was the encouragement of research. Most studies which it initiated were concerned with questions broader than the jurisdictional problems of a particular state agency. Another agency to do research was the California Bureau of Criminal Statistics, established in the office of the Attorney General. It has developed an extensive system for operational service accounting, issued periodic statistical reports, and encouraged broad organizational concern with research questions. Eight special governor's Study Commissions were set up with staff hired for each and with findings that were widely circulated.[2]

In 1957, research departments were organized within both the Department of Corrections and the Department of the Youth Authority. Newsletters and releases are issued periodically to inform Department of Corrections personnel on research activities and their findings. Research has become an important aid to policy making.

This administrative policy enjoyed considerable support among the Department's employees. When asked to express preferences for spending a $100,000 gift, research was ranked second to

[1]Section 6028 of the California Penal Code authorized the conduct of research by the state agencies. See Deering's *Penal Code of the State of California*. San Francisco, California, Bancroft-Whitney Company, 1949.

[2]Each of the following eight commissions collected and analyzed a considerable body of relevant data and made recommendations for action; both interim and final reports were published by the Board of Corrections: a. The Commission of Organized Crime, 1949. b. The Commission of Criminal Law and Procedure—Report issued on June 30, 1949. c. The Commission on Juvenile Justice—Report issued on June 30, 1949. d. The Commission of Adult Correction and Release Procedures—Reports issued on June 30, 1949. e. The Commission of the Social and Economic Causes of Crime and Delinquency—Report issued on June 30, 1949. f. The Commission of Organized Crime—Combined Reports issued in November, 1950. g. The Commission of Correctional Facilities and Services—especially on probation, jails and parole—1957. h. Special Study Commission on Juvenile Justice—November, 1960.

hiring more treatment personnel by the employees. More than one-fifth of all personnel were willing to give research the highest priority among alternate choices for the use of these funds (see Table 18).

TABLE 18

PREFERENCES OF DEPARTMENT OF CORRECTIONS EMPLOYEES
FOR SPENDING A $100,000 GIFT*

(In Per Cent)

	Professional Service Personnel with Advanced Schooling** (N = 337)	All Employees (N = 3,654)
Hire more professional treatment staff (psychiatrists, psychologists, and social workers)	34	31
Hire more research personnel	25	22
Pay merit bonuses to staff who do their work well	2	8
Establish a travel fund for needy dependents of prisoners who could not otherwise visit them	7	7
Build additional recreational facilities for inmates	2	7
Other (specify)	28	22
No answer	2	3

*Responses to question: "Assume you are an administrative assistant to the Director and you are asked to recommend how to spend a gift to the Department of $100,000 to be spent in any manner. What would be your recommendations?"

**Persons with Master's or Doctor's level degree in social work, sociology, psychology, public administration and psychiatry or a Bachelor's degree in education, correctional administration and business administration.

There was far more ambivalence about facing up to the administrative implications of research findings. The great majority of employees expressed a reluctance to recommend interpretation of the research data or publication of the findings, particularly if they were discouraging about the effectiveness of group counseling (see Table 19).

TABLE 19

INTERPRETATION AND COMMUNICATION READINESS OF PROFESSIONALS FOR ENCOURAGING
AND DISCOURAGING EVALUATIVE RESEARCH FINDINGS, CALIFORNIA
DEPARTMENT OF CORRECTIONS*

Recommendation	Correctional Officers (N = 1,470)		Mental Health Personnel (N = 159)	
	Encouraging Finding	Discouraging Finding	Encouraging Finding	Discouraging Finding
Recommend no release of findings at this time	6	10	1	3
Recommend that methodology and sampling techniques be re-examined and that the study be continued to get more information	24	44	31	50
Recommend findings with careful interpretation be released as confidential memo to staff only	10	10	7	7
Recommend that findings with careful interpretation be released as a technical report to a professional journal such as *Journal of Criminal Law and Criminology*	33	20	29	16
Recommend that findings with careful interpretation by agency research specialists be issued to newspapers	20	10	29	20
Recommend that the facts be released to newspapers for interpretation by their own feature writers	6	5	3	2
Unknown	1	1	---	2
Total	100	100	100	100

*Encouraging Finding: "Suppose that a study showed that inmates in group counseling have *less trouble* in prison (violate fewer rules) than those who refused to participate. Assume you are a member of a Department-wide research advisory committee. What would be your recommendations with regard to publicizing the findings? Check one *only*."

Discouraging Finding: "Suppose that a study showed that people in group counseling do *no better* on parole than those who refuse to participate. Assume you are a member of a Department-wide research advisory committee. What would be your recommendation with regard to publicizing this finding? Please check one *only*."

In the Department of Corrections, as in other large organizations, the majority of employees preferred to be tentative about research findings affecting an important agency policy, unless they were supportive of that policy. The employees expressed self-censorship attitudes. Only a minority expressed a willingness to look at all of the evidence and have it widely disseminated. The future of evaluative research will depend on the encouragement by Departmental policy makers of this autonomous minority of Departmental employees.[1]

STABILIZATION OF REFORM MILIEU

In 1931, the sociologist Edwin Sutherland told an assembly of American Prison Association: "Prisoners are the most difficult people to reform and a prison is the worst place in the world in which to reform them." Since 1944, the California Department of Corrections has tried to disprove this conclusion. Evidence of the outcome of prison experience is not easy to come by. But there has been an energetic accumulation of administratively planned changes to transform prisons into correctional institutions. Reform principles have been incorporated into every aspect of the Department's activities, its staff and personnel policies, its management, the architecture of its new institutions, and the kind of treatment programs that have been encouraged. By 1954, an atmosphere of policy-consistency had been created which expressed itself in confidence on the part of many employees that the reform policies were well established and here to stay.

Recognition of California's accomplishment in putting into practice many of the recommended policies of the correctional reform movement has begun to cumulate. The Eighty-sixth Congress of Corrections, in 1956, voted to revise its recently published *Manual of Correctional Standards*.[2] Richard McGee was made the Committee's chariman of the working committee. While over 120 persons with a variety of professional interests and experiences contributed to this revision, the editing was done by the central

---

[1]Joseph W. Eaton: "Symbolic and Substantive Evaluative Research," *Administrative Science Quarterly*, Vol. 6, No. 4, March, 1962.

[2]The American Correctional Association, *op. cit.*

office staff of the California Department of Corrections. Its experiences, practices, and expectations greatly influenced the standards
recommended throughout the *Manual's* six hundred pages covering
every aspect of institutional and parole operations.

Correctional reform is more than a single idea. It is a network
of ideas. They have influenced correctional policy in every state
of the Union. In California, they have been applied with considerable consistency throughout the state prison system. In 1954,
after a decade of reorganization, a nurturant administrative climate
existed that was supportive of comprehensive experimentation
with psychosocial treatment through group psychotherapy and
group counseling. In the next chapter, the pattern emerging from
this program will be described.

Chapter 6

INITIATION

THE EMPHASIS ON GROUP TREATMENT

Between 1944 and 1954 policy makers of the Department of Corrections were preoccupied with the over-all reorganization of the Department, plant expansion, improvements of personnel policy, and updating of every activity. A part of the activity involved the development of treatment programs for individual inmates, but no extraordinary organizational attention was given to this objective.

Throughout the developmental decade, policy makers expressed dissatisfaction with the spasmodic nature of the Department's rehabilitation efforts. Insufficient funds were available to hire professional personnel in large enough numbers to provide therapeutically oriented treatment for all its inmates. And if such funds could have been secured, there was, and still is today, a national shortage of trained people who could be hired.[1] The California Department of Mental Hygiene, which will not hire psychiatric social workers without a Master's degree in social work, had thirty-eight new positions eliminated by the 1960 Legislature. New personnel could not be recruited to fill these vacancies. The number of social workers graduated in California universities was insufficient to meet normal replacement needs and not quite 6 per cent of the number estimated to be required by California agencies during the next ten years.[1] Shortages are probably similar in magnitude in the field of psychology and psychiatry.[2]

---

[1]Liaison Committee of the Regents of the University of California and State Board of Education, *Report of the Advisory Committee on Social Welfare Education,* Berkeley, California, 1961, mimeographed report.

[2]George Albee: Mental Health Manpower Trends: A Report to the Staff Director. Joint Commission on Mental Illness and Health. New York, Basic Books, 1959.

Nationally, professional treatment experts were predisposed to regard a one-to-one therapeutic interaction as the most promising technique, but in the light of the manpower shortage, it was strategic for the Department of Corrections to try out group approaches. There was a good deal of precedent for such programming in correctional settings. By the end of 1950, forty-nine penal institutions reported the use of group treatment programs.[1] Group psychotherapy was being tried even more extensively in the country's state mental hospitals.[2] The idea that correctional institutions should have some form of group treatment as part of their regular program enjoyed national sanction. It was reflected in a rapid increase in the number of institutions offering such programs to their inmates.[3]

As previously mentioned, two differently labeled group treatment programs were given official encouragement in California, group counseling and group psychotherapy. Group psychotherapy was begun in 1947 at San Quentin and blossomed into an institution-wide program at the California Medical Facility after 1950, under the influence of Michael Rosow, M.D., a psychiatric consultant, and Nathaniel Showstack, M.D., the institution's Clinical Director.[4] Group counseling was begun in 1954 at Folsom Prison under the direction of Norman Fenton, Ph.D., a psychologist and the Deputy Director of Classification and Treatment.

GROUP PSYCHOTHERAPY

The California Medical Facility was built as a specialized facility for chronically ill prisoners and those who were mentally

---

[1] Lloyd W. McCorkle: "The Present Status of Group Therapy in United States Correctional Institutions," *International Journal of Group Psychotherapy*, Vol. 3, January, 1953.

[2] J. J. Geller: "Current Status of Group Psychotherapy Practices in State Hospitals for Mental Disease," *Group Psychotherapy*, Vol. 3, August-December, 1950.

[3] Lloyd W. McCorkle and Albert Elias: "The Present Status of Group Therapy in United States Correctional Institutions," *Federal Probation*, Vol. 24, No. 2, 1961.

[4] Nathaniel Showtack: "Group Psychotherapy at the California Medical Facility," Sacramento, California, Department of Corrections, mimeographed report, 1951; also, Nathaniel Showstack, "Preliminary Report on the Psychiatric Treatment of Prisoners at the California Medical Facility," San Predo, California, *American Journal of Psychiatry*, Vol. 112, April, 1956.

disturbed, actively homosexual or who needed a medically controlled environment for other reasons. Its psychiatric staff was too
small to provide individualized therapy for more than a few inmates. As an expedient alternative the clinical director organized
treatment groups of forty to fifty patients meeting regularly once
a week. Their discussions generally were centered around the presentation of a life history given by an inmate volunteer. The sessions
were education-oriented rather than psychologically intensive.

From this beginning the program expanded. The number of
groups increased while their size reduced. This was accomplished
by enlisting the aid of physicians who were not psychiatrists, of
psychologists, of sociologists, and of psychiatric social workers. The
so-called group psychotherapy program which emerged was based
on the following assumptions:

1. Extensiveness of coverage should receive a higher priority
    than intensity of treatment. As the program developed,
    most groups met once a week for an hour and a half and
    included five to eight persons. In principle, the therapists
    would have preferred to meet in small groups and more
    frequently, but there were not enough of them to provide
    even this nominal coverage for all of the inmates willing
    to participate.

2. Group leadership should be restricted to college graduates
    with inclinations for doing therapy. The psychiatric desig-
    nation of "group psychotherapy" was used because all
    group leaders were under the general supervision of the
    clinical director, a psychiatrist, and received occasional
    clinical consultation by a counseling psychoanalyst.

This medically supervised group program at the California
Medical Facility could not service all inmates at Vacaville. Nor
could it be duplicated in other prisons where there were few or no
qualified psychiatrists to provide leadership. Even at Vacaville,
where there were eleven positions for psychiatrists, most of them
were filled by physicians who did not specialize in psychiatry. Psychiatry is a professional specialty with many alternate employment
opportunities. Such physicians are in great demand and can usually
get positions paying more than the top salary level allowable under
California civil service regulations.

Psychologists and social workers have shown more readiness to make their career in the Department of Corrections. Their alternate career opportunities are more restricted than those of psychiatrists. But the combined manpower of these clinically trained persons employed by the prison system could not provide intensive treatment for 23,000 inmates. In 1959, only ninety-seven persons with graduate training in psychology, social work, or psychiatry were employed in the Department.[1] Not all of them were available for doing treatment. Many had full or part-time administrative and supervisory positions.

THE FOLSOM BEACHHEAD

In 1954, Dr. Fenton decided to experiment in the use of non-clinical personnel in a treatment-related function. He was mindful of their lack of training to engage in treatment, but he viewed their easy access to inmates as a resource to be harnessed in support of treatment. He wanted to move in this program, with professionally trained persons when possible and without them, when necessary.

Folsom Prison was chosen as the experimental site. In 1954, this prison had a population of 2,400, most of them older and supposedly hardened criminals. It was surrounded by forbidding stone walls. Its facilities for work programs, education, or recreation were sub-standard. Folsom was twenty-eight miles from headquarters in Sacramento so that Fenton could personally conduct counseling groups without too much loss of time from his busy schedule. It also was a "tough" place run by men who had come from custody ranks. They were highly regarded by "old guard" correctional officers, efficient custodially but skeptical about many of the more treatment-oriented ideas which were coming to the fore in the Department.

The Warden of Folsom was congenial to the experiment. After gaining the approval of the others in the institution's top management, the Deputy Director began the program of group counseling by meeting with fifteen inmates once a week for about two months. They sat in a circle in a large counseling room. Inter-

---

[1]This figure includes persons with at least a Master's degree in social work or psychology and a psychiatric residence in the case of doctors.

ested prison employees, including the Associate Warden, were invited to attend as observers. Two correctional officers (guards), the institutional librarian, and the sociologist volunteered to try their hand at meeting with inmate groups of their own. Fenton served as their consultant, as did the prison's correctional classification officer, a social worker. Towards the end of 1954, the program was expanded. Seventy-one members of the staff participated actively as trainees in the demonstration program. Perhaps another 100 employees attended occasional sessions or special meetings who were not considered trainees to become group leaders.[1]

Fenton's role in directing teaching and counselor consultation was supplemented by the writing of a "How to do it" manual for group leaders and a mental hygiene text book for inmates involved in group counseling. The first provided a common guide to the rapidly growing number of counselors. The second was used by group leaders as an optional text to stimulate discussion and otherwise enrich the program.[2]

There were skeptics, both among the professionally trained treatment people and among old line custodians, but they were not vociferous in their opposition, perhaps because group counseling was given unequivocal administrative support. The Department's Deputy Director of Classification and Treatment personally assumed the role of teacher. Director Richard A. McGee authorized the experiment, and those in charge of Folsom Prison were cooperative. After its feasibility had been demonstrated, an assembly was held of 500 prisoners who had volunteered to be in counseling groups. It was attended by the employees who had been trained as leaders. Director McGee and members of the Adult Authority (Parole Board) were present and expressed their support of the program. After the program became well established many employees came to think that group counseling was a way to get organizational

[1] Norman Fenton: *A Brief Historical Account of Group Counseling in the Prisons of California.* Sacramento, California, Department of Corrections, 1957.

[2] For counselors, Norman Fenton wrote *Correctional Employees Training Manual, No. VII, An Introduction to Group Counseling in Prison.* Sacramento, California, Department of Corrections, 1955; for prisoners, he wrote *What Will Be Your Life?* Sacramento, California, Department of Corrections, 1954. Both texts have subsequently been revised several times. They have been reprinted by the American Correctional Association for distribution throughout the prison world.

recognition, perhaps even a promotion.[1] But when it started at Folsom in 1954, its appeal was more to the venturesome and the innovators who were willing to try the experiment.

Dr. Fenton aroused initial enthusiasm for his idea by suggesting that group counseling might be a way to reform people, a cause for which a number of employees were willing to contribute their own leisure time. It offered custodial, maintenance, educational, and administrative employees involvement in a highly esteemed function—the treatment of inmates. Their work is concentrated in the care and control aspects of the system—regular meals, orderly cell blocks, and absence of escape attempts. Enthusiasm is not easily aroused for these important routines. Group counseling was welcomed as a treatment program with promise of attacking some of the fundamental problems of correctional work. For many months thousands of hours of employee time was donated to group treatment until funds to compensate counselors for overtime could become part of the Department's regular budget.

Group treatment was also relatively economical, a great attraction to prison administrators chronically plagued by tight budgets and shortages of clinically-trained personnel. The per capita cost of being counseled in a group was less than twenty-five cents per session.

CO-EXISTENCE OF DIFFERENT TREATMENT PROGRAMS

The assignment of a task that looked like "therapy" to clinically untrained persons led to two types of apprehension. One was client-centered: would the establishment of group counseling downgrade the over-all Department quality of psychosocial treatment of offenders? The other apprehension was therapist-centered: what would happen to the status of professionals if group counseling could be performed well by clinically-untrained persons?

The *client-oriented* apprehension that counseling groups might damage some of the inmates was not substantiated. No case of overt acting-out behavior, psychotic breakdown, or other form

---

[1]There is evidence that this may have been the case. Readers will recall that group leaders were over-represented among persons whose earnings rose more rapidly than the average employee employed for the same amount of time. For details, see Table 16, page 123.

of pathology could be related to the involvement in a group led by a lay person. On the contrary, prisoners in group counseling were better adjusted to prison life, showed less readiness to escape, and verbally expressed more socially acceptable attitudes than those who received no therapeutically-oriented attention.[1] R. D. Heim found that inmates after counseling expressed less identification with delinquent attitudes and ideas and made more "socially mature" responses.[2]

A survey at Folsom Prison showed that counseled inmates committed only one-half of the number of recorded disciplinary infractions as inmates who had applied for enrollment in group counseling but were still on a waiting list.[3] The counseled men had even fewer—only one-third as many—disciplinary infractions than a second control group, inmates who had *neither* requested nor ever participated in a counseling group.

Inmates in group counseling were less responsive to the antisocial expectations of the inmate culture than those not enrolled in such programs. E. L. R. Roberts reported evidence that there is a "change among group counseling inmates from an attitude indicative of strict compliance with or adherence to the prescriptions of the inmate social system, to one indicating a lesser degree of acceptance of these traditional controls. Also suggested, in the responses of the counselees, was a greater degree of acceptance in their social relationship with other individuals and races."[4]

Personal experiences were reported in every institution supporting the idea that group counseling is a good program. Most group leaders could personally match cases with that reported by Correctional Sergeant S. Palacios about how their own counseling was influencing inmates:

---

[1]Department of Corrections: *Surveys and Studies on Group Counseling.* Sacramento, California, mimeographed memorandum, dated January 28, 1958.

[2]Richard B. Heim: *Changes in Verbalized Attitudes Expressed by Prison Inmates Following Group Counseling.* Claremont, California, Claremont College, Ph.D. dissertation, 1958. His findings did not show, however, that inmates expressed a more insightful picture of themselves than those not exposed to group counseling.

[3]They could not be enrolled because there was a shortage of counselors and space to accommodate all of them.

[4]E. L. R. Roberts: *A Study of the Effects of Group Counseling on Association Choices and Status Ascription Among Inmates at the California State Prison at San Quentin.* San Francisco, Master's Thesis, San Francisco State College, 1960.

"On August 27, 1959, eight California Youth Authority inmates were transferred to the Deuel Vocational Institution because of their incorrigible conduct at other facilities. This group, composed of six Mexicans, one White and one Negro, had been a continual source of disciplinary problems at Paso Robles Camp and Preston. The problems they presented ranged from assaults upon other inmates to attempts to incite a disturbance of major proportions.

"Because of the problems they had caused, it was initially decided to keep them apart from each other during the stay at DVI. In fact, because they were the most incorrigible in the group, two of them were placed in our Adjustment Center.

"As word about their arrival spread throughout the institution, we received reports that the Mexican population felt disturbed over the fact that six of the eight were of Mexican origin, and they were anxious to help them make a good start at DVI. After thorough consideration, it was decided to make arrangements for these six inmates to attend a counseling group composed of Mexican-American inmates who are under the leadership of a Spanish-speaking correctional sergeant. The Mexican inmate who was in the Adjustment Center at that time was also permitted to attend the group. Their response was so promising that we decided to have them enrolled in this counseling group permanently, and they continued to attend regularly.

"Because of their rapid adjustment, we were able to assign four of these inmates to work crews outside of the security area, and the inmate who had originally been assigned to the Adjustment Center was released to the general population, where he too made a good adjustment. To date, only three of this group of six have received disciplinary reports for infraction of rules, and those three reports were minor in nature. All six have continuously earned good work grades. Three were released on parole during the month of November.

"Originally we anticipated a lot of problems collectively and individually from this particular group; especially the six inmates of Mexican origin, since their cultural background, as well as their past institution behavior, provided them with a common interest. Our success with this group was largely due to their enrollment in a counseling group where they were enlightened as to their position in the institution, especially in the eyes of other inmates of the same racial background. They were coun-

seled as to the eventual consequence should they continue to be-
have in an unacceptable manner. They were offered assistance
and guidance and, most of all, encouraged to strive for good conduct."[1]

The *therapist* centered apprehensions remained to be dealt
with. Could group counseling by inexperienced lay persons co-
exist with activity that looked identical, but which was led by professionally trained personnel? There were no data to document
what the differences were and how they would affect inmates participating in groups.

Group counselors were urged not to give warning or threats,
to proffer no advice, or to try suggestion or hypnotism. They were
instructed to be non-directive and to encourage free association by
inmates or spontaneous expression of their thought and feelings.[2]
Nevertheless, it was plausible to assume that full-time clinicians
who had studied therapy for many years would do better in such
work with groups than correctional officers, who changed their
cusodial role for ninety minutes a week to be a counselor.

In spite of these reasons for skepticism about group counseling,
Fenton obtained the support of many clinically trained professionals because of the experimental nature of his innovation. In every
prison but one, he co-opted some of them as teachers and consultants to the lay counselors. Only at the California Medical Facility
at Vacaville he encountered strong opposition.

His plans were considered initially by the staff at Vacaville for
auxiliary use with inmates reported as seemingly unresponsive to
group psychotherapy.[3] Fenton and the members of the Department's psychiatric staff met in the fall of 1955 at a seminar entitled,
"Similarities, Differences and Relationships of Group Counseling
and Group Psychotherapy."[4] The seminar discussed the fact that:

---

[1]Department of Corrections: State of California, *Group Counseling Newsletter,*
Vol. III, No. 4, October, November, December, 1959.

[2]Norman Fenton: *An Introduction to Group Counseling in State Correctional
Service.* Sacramento, California, Department of Corrections, 1957.

[3]Norman Fenton: *A Brief Historical Account of Group Counseling in the Prisons
of California.*

[4]Norman Fenton, Editor: *The Similarities, Differences and Relationships of
Group Counseling and Group Psychotherapy.* Notes from a Departmental Seminar
held at the California Medical Facility, Vacaville, California, October and November,
1955. Sacramento, California, 1956, mimeographed.

. . . other than titles and academic or other training of the personnel conducting the two programs, there is probably no conclusive functional and operative dividing line between group counseling and group psychotherapy. In the first place, group leaders in group counseling differ as do psychotherapists. Some of the latter, who lack training in dynamic psychiatry, tend to be didactic and moralistic in their group work. Some of the former have had courses in group dynamics or in counseling and guidance and have learned to be skillfully permissive and non-directive in their counseling.

A number of counseling demonstration sessions were given at this medically controlled prison, but the idea was not adopted in 1955. The medical staff preferred to expand group therapy sessions, leading ultimately to inclusion of nearly 50 per cent of the inmate population. The Superintendent reported in 1956 that there were eleven full-time therapists, two of them with education in psychiatry, four in medicine, two in clinical psychology, and the remaining three in sociology and psychology. Each carried a load of about 100 patients, with an average of ten per group. Some of these groups were restricted to tubercular, psychotic, narcotic, pre-parolee, or adolescent patients. Otherwise no special effort was made towards achieving homogencity in the composition of the group.[1] Most of them met twice weekly, for an hour. The leaders were given as much supervision as could be provided by the prison's Chief of Professional Services, who was a psychiatrist.

In August 1960, thirty staff members of Vacaville were involved in the treatment program. Of the physicians, only a minority had specialized in psychiatry. All of the non-medical therapists were college graduates, with some graduate work. Their supervision was not intensive, but more therapeutically sophisticated than was being offered the average group counselors.

The psychotherapy program was led by a higher proportion of appropriately trained personnel than group counseling, but in both the majority of leaders were persons who had not completed a clinically oriented academic degree program in psychiatry, psychology, or social work. They did not meet minimum qualifica-

---

[1]M. R. King: "Psychiatric Program of the California Medical Facility," *Proceedings of the American Correctional Association*, New York, 1956.

tions of their profession for doing psychotherapy. This led to more and more questions about the differences in the nature and impact on offenders of group processes led by persons with different educational backgrounds. The use of the terms *therapy* and *counseling* by Departmental employees no longer corresponded to the distinction reported after the Vacaville conference. Psychiatrists and psychologists continued to use the term "group psychotherapy" to describe their work. But the social workers were divided between those who called their work with groups "counseling" and those who called it "therapy." Occasionally employees, who claimed no membership in a professional society and who had no clinical training, designated as "therapy" the meetings they conducted with inmates.

IS TRAINING NEEDED TO DO THERAPY?

The co-existence within the same department of two categories of group treatment that overlap in their theoretical rationale is symptomatic of a general question of concern to all of the helping professions: how does training affect performance? Can men counsel others competently without a professional degree? If so, when and how? Psychologists, social workers, and psychiatrists require graduate training in universities, plus supervised clinical work. Pastoral and marriage counselors vary more widely in what they regard as universally acceptable training. And there also are many persons who do counseling without a professional "license." The most extensive welfare services in the United States—those dealing with the poor on public assistance, the aged on old age assistance programs, and the treatment of juvenile and adult offenders in institutions and on parole—often are the direct responsibility of persons who lack even a college education. Rarely have they completed a course of clinical training in a graduate school.

People who are expected to help others with complex problems they cannot solve on their own require both wisdom and technical knowledge that can be enhanced by appropriate training. At the same time, in any treatment programs manned by semi-skilled or unskilled personnel, individuals with impressive motivation, warmth, and capacity for counseling can be found.

The helping professions lack a scientifically based rationale for making a division of labor between differently trained and untrained employees who offer similar counseling services. Administrators of therapeutic clinics often draw a line on the basis of professionally sanctioned traditions. For instance, in inter-disciplinary child guidance clinics the making of a diagnosis is often restricted to pyschiatrists. Social workers think that cottage parents in an institution for disturbed children require less training than group workers. These distinctions rest more on arrogance than evidence. They may be administratively comfortable, but do not solve the question of just what kind of training contributes to the helping process.

The co-existence of two group treatment programs in one correctional organization has not led to a work conflict between their advocates. On the contrary, the great majority of those who counsel with an academic degree approved of the efforts of those who did counseling without it. Of ninety-seven psychiatrists, psychologists, and social workers with professional degrees,[1] 71 per cent selected psychotherapy and 3 per cent group counscling as the most promising of eight activities "most likely to make the greatest impact on an offender's chances of reformation." Two-thirds of these professionals included group counseling and group psychotherapy among three choices of "most promising" approaches. Only slightly less optimism about the value of group counseling was expressed by those Departmental employees who chose psychotherapy as the "most promising activity for having an impact on offenders." Fifty-five per cent of 615 group therapy enthusiasts included group counseling among their second or third choice.

Confidence in psychotherapy was not reciprocated to the same extent by the 202 persons who selected group counseling as their first choice. Only 30 per cent selected psychotherapy as their second or third choice. Those impressed with the treatment potential of group counseling were more optimistic about the potentialities of educational techniques, particularly vocational education which was mentioned by 67 per cent as their second or third choice.

---

[1]Included were twenty-two psychiatrists with a Doctoral degree, thirty psychologists with a Master's degree and three with a Ph.D., forty-one social workers with a Master's degree, and one with a Doctoral degree.

In the light of the tolerant and optimistic assessment of most professionally trained therapists towards the fledgling group counseling program, it is not surprising that a gradual de-emphasis on the supposed theoretical differences between group therapy and group counseling took place. In 1960, under the influence of a new medical superintendent, group counseling was introduced at Vacaville as an aid and supplement to the on-going group therapy program.

What started as an "experiment" at Folsom in January, 1954, grew within two years into a department-wide program of 375 counseling groups with 4,957 inmates. In addition, about 1,000 prisoners were reported to be in group psychotherapy at the California Medical Facility at Vacaville. Group treatment thus became the Department's most extensive treatment activity.

There was a great deal of enthusiasm for this development, both in the Department and in correctional circles all over the country when the program was new. It had promise of accomplishing something that previously tried treatment techniques failed to do: the involvement of large numbers of inmates in a therapeutically-oriented experience. In 1959, group counseling was thought by just over half of the employees to influence inmates to break fewer prison rules and to bring about basic personality change. But the staff were more uncertain that it would reduce inmate recidivism after leaving prison (Table 2, page 55), although they allowed for the possibility that this could happen. Only 15 per cent of the employees were willing to say that this hope was false.

Optimism was highest among those actively engaged in treatment. There was less among inactive group leaders or those who had never led a group. The active leaders were strongly in disagreement with the statement "Group counseling has no proven effects on anyone or anything." While most of those who were not leading groups also disagreed with this deprecatory view, many more checked "uncertain" as describing their reaction (see Table 20).

Some of the group treatment enthusiasts spoke of their hopes as if they were evidence of accomplishment. But those administratively responsible for the program had a more scientific orientation. They recognized that the leaders lacked the training, which

TABLE 20

STAFF RESPONSES TO THE QUESTION, "GROUP COUNSELING HAS NO PROVEN EFFECTS
ON ANYONE OR ANYTHING"

(In Per Cent)

		Responses	
Involvement	*True*	*Uncertain or No Response**	*False*
Persons Active in Treatment			
Group Therapy (N = 63)	3	17	80
Group Counseling (N = 655)	6	19	75
Persons Who Used to Do Treatment			
Group Therapy (N = 23)	13	30	57
Group Counseling (N = 514)	10	25	65
Persons Who Never Did Group Counseling or Therapy (N = 2,380)	9	32	59

*In no category did the percentage of non-respondents exceed 3 per cent.

they viewed as important. But they preferred untrained group leaders to no group leaders at all. Their involvement, even if it were not to have much of a therapeutic impact on inmates, would at least make the employees more identified with a treatment point of view. Group counseling helped to co-opt educators and custody employees to support the theory of reform. The therapy-oriented policy makers made it possible for important and powerful elements of the organization to take a key place in this new effort. Anyone with enthusiasm and good will was welcomed. Group counseling was an innovation that did not exclude people. This co-optation process probably averted what might otherwise have become a focus of rivalry among the different Departmental programs.[1]

Those responsible for nurturing the Department's program did not close their eyes to the existence of many unresolved questions. They acknowledged that no matter how dedicated the efforts of group leaders, evaluation of their success would ultimately have

[1]The cooptation process is well described by Philip Selznick, *TVA and the Grass Roots, A Study in the Sociology of Formal Organizations.* Berkeley, Los Angeles, University of California Press, 1953.

to be in terms of their impact on inmates. Research was encouraged in the hope that evidence would turn up that group counseling is an effective technique of prisoner rehabilitation. Before and while evidence was piling up, they strove to perfect the program's operations. This was a prerequisite to meaningful research on how group counseling and group psychotherapy affect inmates. There first had to be a well developed program that could be subjected to research. In consequence, steps were taken to build group treatment procedures solidly into the Department's administrative machinery.

Chapter 7

INSTITUTIONALIZATION

AN IDEA BECOMES A PROGRAM

Institutionalization refers to the development of regularized procedures to accomplish organizational objectives on a continuing basis. It includes such actions as the appointment of permanent staff, provisions of a budget, and fitting arrangement for the innovation into the administrative machinery. Organizationally sanctioned values are attached to the innovation. This is what occurred with group treatment in the Department of Corrections.

Administrative bottle-necks to the development of an institution-wide counseling program were overcome by co-optation. Dr. Fenton did not impose his views, but relied on demonstration and education to persuade employees to participate in this venture.[1] Counseling leadership resulted in special organizational attention for the employee. His role was brought to the attention of the immediate supervisor, the Warden and Director McGee. A personal letter of appreciation was sent after an employee became a group counselor made out for the signature of the Warden or Superintendent, with a copy to Director McGee and the employee's personnel file. At regular intervals, additional letters of appreciation were sent.

Superintendents, wardens, and other high echelon administrators were encouraged to become personally as well as administratively involved in the development of group treatment in their own institutions. Fenton shared authorship and the limelight with a Superintendent and a Warden of two of the State's prisons, when he presented a first report on California's program of group coun-

---

[1]For more details, see Norman Fenton, *A Brief Historical Account of Group Counseling in the Prisons of California,* 11-27.

seling to the American Correctional Association.[1] Employees at the Associate Warden level wrote the progress reports of group counseling in most of the prisons.[2] When our survey was made in 1959, 48 per cent of the policy makers and 45 per cent of the custody administrators reported they had personally led a counseling group.

PERMANENT STAFFING

Group counseling was becoming too extensive an activity to be administered out of the brief-case of the Department's Deputy Director. A full-time Coordinator of Group Counseling, stationed at the Sacramento headquarters, was appointed in 1957. His duties were: to provide instruction to institutional personnel leading counseling groups; to encourage continuous development of the various group counseling texts, manuals, and instructions; to audit counseling groups to insure that sound, uniform, and proper standards were being followed; to evaluate and analyze the program to insure continual improvements; to make regular progress reports of the counseling program; to maintain liaison with the Adult Authority and other administrative personnel; and to integrate group counseling with other aspects of the Departmental treatment program.

The Coordinator was authorized to recruit a staff of Group Counseling Program Supervisors in the major prisons. Since no funds were at first available, an interim part-time staff was selected from the ranks of correctional classification officers who were already employed. At the same time, the Department of Finance and the Legislative Analyst for the Joint Legislative Budget Committee were asked to recommend legislative approval for a full-time staff member in each prison to develop treatment for the following reasons:

1. The claim was made that group counseling has been demonstrated as a control device with treatment potentials. Research findings were used to support this assertion.

---

[1] Allen Cook, Norman Fenton and Robert A. Heinze: "Group Counseling in Prison," *Proceedings of the Eighty-fifth Annual Congress of Corrections of the American Correctional Association,* New York, 1955.

[2] See, for instance, the *Group Counseling Newsletter,* April-May, 1959.

2. Evidence was cited that the operation of group counseling in each institution had become a full-time job. A "conservative" formula, sixty counselors for each supervisor, was suggested to provide proper supervision.
3. The economy aspect of group counseling was stressed. The cost per hour of counseling was estimated at about eighteen cents. This was an under-estimate, particularly if the administrative and training costs of the program are pro-rated.
4. It was pointed out that group counseling is the only service offering sustained help with social and personal problems for the majority of inmates.[1]

The Legislature agreed. Program Supervisor positions were authorized. The salary range was from $556 to $676 in 1960, a rate of pay somewhat higher than that of Correctional Lieutenant and below that of Correctional Captain. The Program Supervisors thus stood high in the organizational hierarchy.

The job description called for multiple skills, a hard-to-find combination of teaching, treatment, supervisory, and administrative skills. The supervisors were expected to conduct in-service training classes for correctional personnel who had never functioned in a group treatment role. They also were to be available as consultants to both the group leaders and the inmates involved as clients. Towards this end, they had to be capable in counseling about complex personal problems and in recommending ways for handling such problems in a group setting. Along with these technical-professional tasks, the Program Supervisors were expected to perform many quasi-administrative functions, such as the recruitment of new leaders, the filling of vacancies when a group leader had to be absent, and the assignment of each inmate to the most appropriate group for him. Each Program Supervisor was responsible for as many as sixty groups. He had to schedule meetings, find room to hold them, fill out forms, and write periodic reports.

It was generally easier to find persons who could meet the administrative expectations than perform the teaching and clinical supervisory functions. Civil Service regulations limited recruitment for these new posts from within the organization. The exist-

---

[1]California Department of Corrections, *Justification, Group Counseling Supervisors.* Sacramento, California, September 5, 1957, mimeographed.

ing manpower pool of correctional counselors who had been hired to work with individual inmates included few persons with completed advanced academic training in one of the treatment fields—psychology, social work, or psychiatry. Those who had such qualifications tended to rise quickly to even more responsible administrative posts than those of Program Supervisors. Administrative realities thus had the effect that Program Supervisors were recruited largely from among correctional counselors at the Number I pay level. Most of them found it easier to do the administrative aspects of their job than to teach, diagnose, and supervise group treatment.

The Department of Corrections made group counseling a major activity by assigning a full-time staff to its nurture and development. But by providing only a limited number of supervisors, about one for every sixty groups, and by limiting their recruitment to personnel already in the manpower pool of the Department of Corrections, these jobs became primarily administrative in their orientation. The lay group counselors did not have experience of their own to draw on. They were quite dependent on leadership provided by the Program Supervisors. Here and there, the men selected for these posts could furnish such leadership. But in several institutions this was not possible. Supervision became more a matter of form than substance.

The Coordinator of Group Counseling in Sacramento recognized this gap. He, therefore, spent much time traveling from institution to institution in order to hold in-service sessions.

ORGANIZATIONAL INTEGRATION

In each institution, group counseling became a regular activity in which personal contact between inmates, and between inmates and staff, was encouraged. At the California Institution for Men at Chino, the time of 3:00 to 4:20 p.m. each Friday was set aside for group meetings. Leaders were instructed to keep attendance lists so that unexcused absentees could be interviewed by the Group Counseling Supervisor. A group counseling building was outfitted, with acoustically balanced rooms which were freshly painted, decorated and refloored. The building also contained two offices and a room for individual interviews.

Top level administrative attention was given to make a full schedule of group meetings possible by rearranging the schedule of other activities. Correctional captains were often designated as Group Counseling Liaison Officers, responsible for seeing that leaders met their groups regularly in the best possible space. They also arranged for a substitute leader in the event that the regular one was indisposed or otherwise occupied.

Space is always at a premium in prisons. Most of them were designed for fewer persons than they now house. In several prisons and all forestry camps groups have to use classrooms or meet in make-shift areas in workshops, industrial areas, corridors, cell-blocks, or storage rooms. In pleasant weather foremen of work crews meet with their inmates in a suitable location outdoors.[1]

An annual group counseling award luncheon is held in most prisons. On these occasions, the newly graduated class of counseling leaders is accorded recognition by the Superintendent, members of the Adult Authority, and representatives of the Central Office in Sacramento. Pioneer and long-term counselors are given recognition for their efforts.

For the Department as a whole, a manual of policies and procedures was issued in 1956 and revised in 1961. Statistical reports are prepared periodically showing what "progress" has been made in recruiting larger numbers of leaders and inmate participants. A *Group Counseling Newsletter* is issued periodically to report about the experiences of counselors and to review new books and articles. It also includes testimonial articles by employees and administrators expressing their conviction that group counseling is good for every inmate and that the faster it grows, the better it will be for the entire Department.

The Department allocated resources and personnel to increase the access of inmates throughout the entire prison system to a group treatment program. Provisions were made for continuous recruitment and indoctrination of group leaders. But what could be done

---

[1]Norman Fenton: *Group Counseling, A Preface to Its Use in Correctional and Welfare Agencies.* Sacramento, California, the County Project in Correctional Methods, Institute for the Study of Crime and Delinquency, 1961.

fell short of its own reorganizational standards. There were limitations in funds to hire specialists, and a shortage of trained specialists, which made them hard to recruit even when funds were available. Awareness of these limitations was balanced psychologically by an emphasis on the idea "Let's do the best we can. Some treatment is better than none." This writer found that officials, when talking about research, could freely entertain unresolved questions regarding the validity of the present treatment program. But when acting in the role of administrators or counseling leaders, they emphasized its newistic aspects—its hopes and aspirations. This source of confidence helped to sustain their interest. Their intellectual skepticism was balanced by a belief that, given time to perfect the program, research would prove that it could make a significant contribution to correctional effectiveness.

Chapter 8

FORMALISM AND DECAY

EVIDENCE OF FORMALISM

Policy makers avow the principle that no treatment procedure, no matter how well established, is beyond the need of being tested by research. Research efforts are encouraged, both by outsiders and by the Department's research staff. Administrators express confidence in the program, particularly when necessary to get budgetary support. But this is done with the acknowledgment that the program's long range effects are as yet unknown.

Facts such as these support the hypothesis that group counseling is a *scientific* reform movement. But its empirical orientation does not protect it from contagion by formalism. There are employees who do counseling as a matter of form, to get the activity on their personnel record, or to receive overtime payments. There are many who do counseling without the skills to do it, and without much concern regarding their lacks. Some administrators seem more impressed by quantitative evidence of the growth and volume of the program than with efforts aimed at improving its quality.

Correctional officers and administrators have schedules which are subject to changes in assignment, working hours, or day off. These changes may obligate counselors at least temporarily to drop their group. Some of these group leaders take their roles rather lightly. Others conduct routinized bull sessions. They have no theory to guide their practice. The word "treatment" has become a positive symbol which is used quite loosely. Counselors receive recognition for their activity rather than what can be demonstrated about its impact on offenders. Conversation between inmates in the presence of a staff cannot be presumed to have inherently therapeutic value. Treatment is an empty symbol if it is used to designate actions which lack its substance, such as diagnostic skill and leadership ability to influence individuals or a group to accomplish a specified objective.

Inmates have used group counseling to acquire a new vocabulary which does not necessarily reflect a change in personality or behavior after release. There is a high turnover in inmate participation. Some feign interest to get credit for good intentions. Quite a few just "volunteer" before their Adult Authority hearing and then drop out soon thereafter. Adult Authority members have reported that they used to have many inmates come up for parole hearing claiming innocence—to have had a "bum beef." Now it is more common for men to admit their guilt. They explain that they did not "understand themselves" and that they are "acquiring insight." They are using the treatment ideology to "con" the Adult Authority, hoping for a more favorable parole consideration.

BUREAUCRATIC RITUALISM

With the establishment of twelve Departmental positions as *Group Counseling Coordinators,* the program became a basis for new jobs. The new positions required a staff capable of teaching and inspiring lay persons to become involved in group treatment activities. The national supply of such personnel is small. Civil Service regulations require that these posts be filled by promoting personnel already in the Department. Clinicians that met the qualifications are in short supply. The demand for them has grown much faster than the supply. This has resulted in a reduction in the training standards of those employed in at least one of the Department's key treatment units, the Reception-Guidance Centers at San Quentin and Chino. In 1952, there was a staff of ten correctional counselors with graduate degrees or their equivalent. In 1956, Reception-Guidance Center personnel had expanded to twenty clinicians, but only six of them had graduate degrees or their equivalent. Three of them had not graduated from college.

The reduction of academic standards affected the quality of the diagnostic work done according to Winslow Rouse, a social scientist and Associate Superintendent who investigated this matter.[1] He rated fifty cases, prepared in October, 1949, at the Reception-Guidance Center at San Quentin and compared them to 100 cases in 1956, fifty from San Quentin and fifty from Chino. He concluded there was a marked decline in quality of the diagnostic documents between 1949 and 1956, although the size of reports remained approximately the same.

Winslow Rouse's findings were similarly critical of vocational counseling done at the Reception-Guidance Centers. He judged it as being "relatively worthless to the inmates and the Department because those (clinicians) assigned to the task lacked specialized education and training or were under such great pressure from a variety of other duties. The same conclusion was applicable to religious activities. Most prisoners were not assessed regarding their religious motivation and potential while entering the institution. A few individual evaluations were prepared by students, serving as religious interns. But they lacked both training and supervision.

It is surprising in the light of such shortages of personnel that some of the Coordinators of group counseling who were recruited were outstanding individuals. They were so outstanding that they soon found themselves promoted out of these posts. Others chosen for these posts lacked many of the qualifications to fulfill the varied and different roles as teachers, inspirers, and administrators. They tend to stress the administrative aspects. They have shown more concern with giving the appearance that groups are meeting than with the substance of what goes on when groups do meet. They tend to be apprehensive about criticism of the group treatment program rather than expecting it as an inherent part of their job, a challenge to be dealt with.

The nature of recruitment of group leaders contributes to routinization of the program. Alfred H. Katz, in a study of group counselors of two prisons, found that one-fifth of his sample of leaders became active after being asked by their immediate superior or by the institutional supervisor of group counseling. Some got

---

[1]Winslow Rouse: *A Report on the Nature and Quality of the Clinical Diagnostic Work (Other Than Psychiatric) of the Reception Guidance Centers.* Sacramento, California, California Department of Corrections, typed report, dated December 18, 1956.

into the program under the not quite accurate supposition that this was a normal and expected component of their jobs. In both institutions, the majority of group leaders had more appropriate motivation. Only a few of the leaders reported getting professional supervision to help them handle problems of their counselees. About one-third of the leaders wanted more supervision than they were receiving. Enthusiasm for the program was significantly lower at one of the institutions, where there also was less supervision. Only a minority of the sample attended group meetings at which the program supervisor led discussions of problems common to several counseling groups. This finding is not consistent with the Department's policy which states that every group counselor is to be given in-service training.[1]

TREATMENT SKEPTICISM

Even more fundamental than administrative problems in developing a viable and vital treatment program is the question of who can be treated under the coercive conditions of imprisonment and on parole. There were indications that many patients who came to the Los Angeles psychiatric clinic for parolees were unmotivated for psychotherapy. While the physical presence of the patients could be assured for about 90 per cent of the appointments, this is not by itself a guarantee that the parolees would be influenced to enhance their self-control and capacity for socially acceptable behavior. Little is known about the differential impact of such "imposed" treatment on different categories of offenders.[2]

Similar questions about treatability arise with respect to group counseling. Among both leaders and inmates, the novelty of counseling wore off. There were some with little optimism about its effectiveness. The 34 per cent of the custody administrators, 12 per cent of the correctional officers, 13 per cent of the educators and researchers, and 15 per cent of the maintenance men who had dropped their work with counseling groups were somewhat less

---

[1]Alfred H. Katz: *Self Perception of Their Roles by Group Counseling Leaders in a Correctional System.* Los Angeles, California, California Study for Correctional Effectiveness, March, 1961, unpublished manuscript.

[2]Albert Labin and Joseph W. Eaton: "Group Psychotherapy for Criminal Offenders," *California Medicine,* Vol. 88, January, 1958.

willing to ascribe treatment potential to this activity than were those still actively engaged in counseling.

For an important minority of group treatment people the activity was a routine. Five psychotherapists (8 per cent) and 156 group counseling leaders (24 per cent) had little confidence in what they were doing. They included neither group treatment method among their three choices of program believed to have "the greatest impact on an offender's chances of reforming." Included among these treatment skeptics were 7 per cent of the professionally trained clinicians—three psychiatrists, three psychologists, and one social worker.

The group treatment programs expanded in spite of skepticism that they could meet their stated objectives. And there were some who were more than just skeptical. They lacked all confidence in what they were doing. Five per cent of the active group psychotherapists and 8 per cent who were doing counseling expressed the point of view that "group counseling has no proven effect on anything or anyone."

OPPOSITION TO RESEARCH

It is one thing for the Director to express the belief that in corrections, as in most fields, progress usually means change. Today's care in medicine may be rated comparatively ineffective tomorrow. A promising rehabilitative technique today may be disregarded next year.

It is quite another thing to be a lower echelon career man in charge of one of these techniques. He sees fewer alternatives for shifting from one technique to another, if what he does were to prove superfluous or ineffective. Parole supervision, for instance, often is a routine. With the parole officer involved in report writing, staff meetings, and the almost daily emergency case, the average parolee can expect little counseling and supervision from his agent. Research into just what he gets has been resisted at many operating levels. The Adult Authority (Parole Board) has to make politically charged decisions about when to allow an offender to return to the community as a parolee. Before each case is heard, voluminous records about each case are compiled. They should be read, discussed, and analyzed, for the decision to be made about a parole date is of great importance to the offender and his community. But the pressure of work is such that four and even more cases are reviewed per hour. There is not enough time to read the written reports and discuss them thoroughly, all the more since part of each hearing is used to give the offender time to plead his side of the case, usually a plea for an early parole date.

One way out of this dilemma is to pay lip-service to the value of doing research, but to oppose many of its procedures. When research occurs, operating personnel function in a fish-bowl atmosphere. Conditions which some will regard as "personal" shortcomings will be noted. The average employee does not welcome research as part of his own job. He is doubtful that it pays off. He prefers to be let alone, to do his job, without being under a research limelight. There is barely suppressed glee in many circles when the researchers make an error, their interpretations can be criticized, or their findings are inconclusive.

Ritualistic and routinized elements in the Department's treatment program are a normal by-product of organizational expansion. Formalism occurs in every social movement as it becomes stabilized, when the spark of innovators becomes the substance of a job description, on the basis of which many men have to be recruited. The crucial element is not that formalism occurs, but how much it pervades the organization. Is it sufficiently pronounced to undermine the essence of the treatment by substituting for it a routine of meetings that look like therapy but are without impact on the participants? Are new programs just new labels for the same old routine? Such conditions would even actually bring about disrepute and disillusionment.

Routinization is a natural by-product of all administration. It is not so extensive as to stifle genuine innovation. Formalism and decay can be contained in a social movement when leaders view them as trends to be corrected rather than to be explained away. They are being counteracted by a strong predisposition on the part of the leadership against settling for the mere existence of activities that look like treatment. The Department is sponsoring and encouraging research (including this study) to evaluate on-going treatment efforts in terms of "hard" evidence of their impact on inmates, while in prison and on parole.

Chapter 9

REORGANIZATION

SCIENCE APPLIED TO ADMINISTRATION

Formalism and routinization are not likely to go unchallenged in an organization where three out of five policy makers disagreed with a statement in our questionnaire that "by and large, conditions in all institutions I know about are as good as they can be, considering the type of prisoners that have to be kept there" (see Chart 6, page 113). It was rare for employees to oversimplify their judgments of individual programs as either a "success" or a "failure." Far more common was the application of the *partial gains* concept as a criterion for assessing change. Progress in penal treatment, it was believed, would be a matter of small steps forward rather than giant strides and total solutions. Innovations could, therefore, be criticized without being abandoned. While policy makers would derive encouragement from a small, but statistically significant reduction of recidivism rates of inmates involved in one form of treatment, they continued in search of new, more dramatically effective techniques.

FROM GROUP TO TOTAL MILIEU TREATMENT

In the year before his retirement from the Department of Corrections, Dr. Fenton turned his attention to a related, but more sociological treatment program: counseling with the families of prisoners. This project, financed by the Rosenberg Foundation of San Francisco, began in 1957.[1]

Group counseling concentrates on changing the individual

---

[1]The project was extended at the time of Dr. Fenton's retirement in the summer of 1958 to include all institutions in the Department of Corrections.

inmates; family counseling, however, is an effort to influence the milieu to which the prisoner returns after his release. Family counseling proceeds from the hypothesis that inmates can be helped to adjust to prison life and to society upon their release through work with their families and close associates. The process involves casework by a parole officer with an inmate's family regarding the problems likely to arise after a man is released. His wife may be invited to attend pre-parole group counseling sessions held at the prison.

A comprehensive report of this demonstration program appeared two years after its initiation.[1] Before the ink was dry on Fenton's report, Director McGee appointed a Departmental committee to "review our experiences with the family counseling project and determine if activities can be incorporated into an on-going program."[2]

Experimentation with an alternate, though not conflicting program was paralleled within the Department by modifications of group treatment procedures. Some counselors began to meet with larger units of twenty to fifty persons. This decision was influenced by a theory that was gaining attention: group counseling might not have much of a psychological impact on the individual offender; rather it is a mechanism to assist in the establishment of better social relationships between inmates and staff members.

This shift in emphasis, to group counseling as an educational technique, was part of the trend to introduce therapeutically-oriented policies in every aspect of the prison environment. Milieu treatment became the newest of key *new* ideas. Its organizational glamour was replacing the old-*new* program of the late 1950's— ninety minutes a week of group treatment.

Dr. Maxwell Jones, the British charismatic exponent of the milieu-treatment idea, was invited to Sacramento to serve as a consultant. His book, *The Therapeutic Community,* has been read by many clinically-oriented Departmental employees.[3] One of his

---

[1]Norman Fenton: *The Prisoner's Family.* Palo Alto, California, Pacific Books, 1959.

[2]Department of Corrections, *Report of Departmental Committee on Family Counseling Project,* June 17, 1959; and *Final Report of Departmental Committee on Family Counseling Project.* Sacramento, California, September 17, 1959, mimeographed.

[3]Maxwell Jones: *The Therapeutic Community,* New York, Basic Books, 1953.

young disciples, Dennie L. Briggs,[1] was encouraged by the Superintendent of the California Institution for Men to organize the "Pilot
Rock" forestry camp along therapeutic community lines. The importance attached to this idea is underlined by the fact that Briggs
was given this responsible assignment while he was still on probationary Civil Service status. Administrators of other institutions
were quick to sense the possible significance of this *new* idea of
treatment and asked for permission to use Mr. Briggs as consultant.

The therapeutic community idea had been discussed in mental
hygiene circles for many years. It was getting increasing attention
throughout California. Special training institutes were held in the
Veterans Administration and in institutions of the Department of
Mental Hygiene. Earlier, the United States Navy had permitted
Dr. Harry A. Wilmer to conduct experiments of the therapeutic-
community type.[2] In the late 1950's the Department of Corrections
headquarters in Sacramento gave more and more official encouragement to this approach as a supplement—or on occasion as an
alternative—to smaller counseling groups. The group counseling
coordinator expressed this in an editorial of the *Group Counseling
Newsletter* at the end of 1959:

> Many group counselors will be puzzled by the large size of
> the daily groups reported by Associate Superintendent Hacker in
> this issue. In therapeutic community programs, as developed by
> Dr. Maxwell Jones in Belmont, England, Dr. Bean in Utrecht,
> Holland, Dr. Harry Wilmer in Oak Knoll Navy Hospital and
> many other hospitals, there are many types of groups including
> large living groups, small therapy groups, work groups, activity
> groups and committees of patients and staff members. One spe-
> cial value of the larger groups, such as Mr. Hacker describes, is
> that they include all personnel and inmates connected with a
> living unit and concentrate on the immediate interpersonal prob-
> lems. Another value is that they are being held at a critical time,
> when the men first come to prison.
>
> We have personally visited the large living groups at the
> C.I.M. Guidance Center seven times and have been impressed

---

[1]Dennie L. Briggs and Frank L. Rundle: "Beginnings of a Therapeutic Community," *U. S. Armed Forces Medical Journal*, Vol. III, No. 6:811-819.

[2]Harry A. Wilmer: *Social Psychiatry in Action.* Springfield, Thomas, 1958.

with the seriousness of the discussions and the attentive way that the large group of up to one hundred followed the contributions of each person. We have also been impressed with the teamwork of Heim, Hamilton, Briggs, Lindbloom and the others who have been involved. All personnel get together immediately after the meeting, which we believe is the best possible way to study group processes.

Associate Superintendent Lloyd, Tehachapi, also discusses a living group program that occurs at a critical time, namely, the six months or more before inmates are released. We have been impressed with the way Mr. Lloyd and his staff have planned and initiated this program, utilizing existing personnel, giving them broadened responsibilities requiring additional skills.[1]

The milieu treatment theory has an implication that is flattering to almost all prison employees. It suggests that everything, not just counseling, can be important, whether it is supervising a work crew or counting inmates to check their presence. Milieu treatment is less psychologically skewed than group treatment and makes more allowance for reform through environmental and educational intervention. It holds out the possibility of therapeutic potential for the work of every employee.

The broadening represented by the shift from group treatment to milieu treatment documents the decline of newistic enthusiasm for the group counseling idea. While this activity has been related to improvements in the adjustment of inmates to prison life, there is no evidence that their behavior after release from prison has been significantly affected. The scientific orientation of people in the Department of Corrections has not allowed group counseling enthusiasts to ignore these facts.

Group counseling, like other forms of psychosocial treatment used in prisons, is not well validated. Walter C. Bailey's extensive review of research in this field concludes that:

. . . evidence of the effectiveness of correctional treatment is inconsistent, contradictory and of questionable reliability. If one were to eliminate from the "successful outcome reports" all studies characterized by questionable research methodology and

---

[1]Robert M. Harrison: *Group Counseling Newsletter,* Vol. III, October, November, December, 1959, No. 4.

procedures, the percentage of successful outcome based on reliably valid evidence would be small indeed.[1]

The uncertainty in which the results of correctional treatment are shrouded is only a special case of the more generalized lack of hard evidence regarding the effectiveness of psychosocial treatment techniques. But the Department of Corrections differs from most mental health agencies in its high degree of concern with reducing the area of uncertainty through research and experimentation.

That group treatment is not *the* solution was always recognized. The Department's broader basis for treatment planning took concrete expression when it established what has hopefully been designated as the "Increased Correctional Effectiveness" program (I.C.E.). It is an omnibus plan, combining expanded versions of already on-going activities with several hitherto untried features.

1. Grouping of inmates and parolees for involvement in different varieties of correctional treatment on a problem basis, such as pre-parole groups, mixed narcotic groups, and special behavior problem groups. In one prison, there is a group of American-Indians which discusses legal, cultural, and welfare problems.

2. Greater utilization of community and family resources in planning for the release of inmates. At San Quentin, for instance, an experiment was initiated in line with the theory that group counseling can strengthen marriage ties. Two inmate groups will be compared. The wives of one of them are also being counseled by a social worker employed by the Jewish Committee for Personnel Service in San Francisco.[2] After release from prison, the groups of parolees will be studied and their adjustment to parole will be compared.

3. Establishment of an "Increased Correctional Effectiveness Unit." In May of 1961, a unit of sixty-six men was set up at San Quentin. It was housed in a construction dormitory, outside the prison security wall system. The resident inmates are required to put in a full day's work. At designated hours in the evening, four times a week, they meet in large groups to talk about adjustment problems. Labor leaders, law enforcement,

---

[1]Walter C. Bailey: *"How Corrective Is Correctional Treatment?"* University of California at Los Angeles, California Study for Correctional Effectiveness, School of Public Health, 1960, unpublished manuscript.

[2]*Group Counseling Newsletter,* Vol. III, April-May, 1959.

community and parole officials are invited from time to time to address the group and discuss problems raised by its members. The men also meet in small groups, twice weekly, under the leadership of correctional counselors, custodial staff, and work supervisors. Members of the immediate families of inmates are invited to attend sixty to ninety days prior to the inmate's release.

Similar pre-release units are being set up at other penal institutions. A training manual, *Increased Correctional Effectiveness,* is being written.[1]

4. A system of temporary return to prison of parolees. When a parolee gives evidence of maladjustment on parole, he can be returned to prison for a short period without losing his parole status. He is returned just long enough to regain self-control. This control device is most often used with drug addicts.

5. Study of these new programs to answer the question: "Are they really more effective?" Reliance is placed on three types of designs:

 a. Descriptive studies of what is being done.

 b. Control group studies.

 c. Use of Base Expectance Rates to compare the experience of any inmate against the average performance of similar inmates.

APPLIED PAROLE PREDICTION

For more than thirty years social scientists have studied the experience of inmates on parole to calculate statistical probabilities that a prisoner with a given criminal history, family background, age, education, and other characteristics would be able to adjust satisfactorily to parole. Like life insurance rates, parole prediction uses the experience of a given population with well-identified characteristics to forecast how an individual is likely to perform. The method is to calculate indices or base expectancies for each characteristic, by weighting it with its statistical relationship to parole performance. A study is in process of 911 parolees, who have been supervised by officers with small caseloads, in *Special Intensive Parole Units.* Their experience is being compared with that of 2,806 men who have had routine parole supervision. The personal characteristics and prison experiences of the men who did signifi-

---

[1]*Correctional Review*, Vol. 16, No. 4, June 13, 1961.

cantly better on parole and those who did significantly worse will be used to predict the adjustment of each man after his release from prison.

Base expectancy rates, once calculated, can be corrected periodically as the experience of prisoners on parole changes. The rates can be used to compare the performance of inmates in an experimental program, like the "Increased Correctional Effectiveness" Units to that of the total prison population. This research mechanism did not exist when group treatment programs were first adopted.

Prisoners whose family background, age, type of crime, prison record, and the rest are like those who were good parole risks are likely to be paroled early and without intensive parole supervision. Those who have characteristics like the inmates with high expectance rates of failure may also be released early, but under a program of intensive parole supervision under officers with a caseload of thirty-five instead of the more normal load of sixty to seventy inmates.

EXPERIMENTAL RELEASE PROCEDURES

The rationale for group treatment is shifting from primary emphasis on its potential for changing inmate personality to an emphasis on changing his social skills. In pursuit of this role-training goal, a number of additional new avenues of action are being considered. Among them are Pre-Release Living Units. Inmates with relatively short sentences can be assigned to such units directly from the Reception Guidance Center without ever entering a regular prison. They will be able to see their family, employers, parole officers, prospective employers, and public officials more easily than regular prison inmates.

Men can be returned to such pre-release units without losing parole status if they are found to be drinking excessively, having serious family or employment difficulties, or showing disorganization in general living routine. Such preventive institutionalization can protect them until they feel ready once more to try again "life on the outside." The objective of these units is to help men to strengthen their internal controls over their behavior by being given considerable responsibility for dealing with normal problems of everyday living while in a penal institution.

For parolees with no, or unhappy family ties, Half-Way Houses (semi-institutional settings) were proposed. They could provide physical and emotional shelter against parole failure. Residents would be free to leave as they please, but would return at night to a group in which their parole adjustment difficulties could be discussed with counselors and other men. These shelters would be run by voluntary agencies. Half-Way Houses would provide a locale in which psychosocial treament could be furnished on a regular basis. In addition to individual and group treatment, the residents of these shelters would furnish each parolee with a potential reference group of persons who understand his adjustment problems.

These newer ideas, like group treatment and vocational education before them, are only promising. Their potential as a partial solution is re-enforced by the ideology of *newism*. But before too long, the new experiments of milieu treatment will have to be supported by evidence of effectiveness if they are to survive the challenge of alternative programs. Researchers, administrators, and budget analysts are already concerned with the collection of evidence to justify milieu treatment techniques. An ideology which says *everything* can be therapeutic still does not explain which actions have more or less potential. There always are limits on what an organization can do. Not every program can be expanded indefinitely. There is neither money nor staff, nor do the prisoners have time to be involved in all programs thought to be good for them. The milieu theory does not provide clear-cut guide lines to choose between the alternate reform activities that are now encouraged in prisons.

INSTITUTIONALIZATION OF INNOVATION

Program development is on its way to being institutionalized. Milton Burdman, who succeeded Norman Fenton as Chief of Classification and Treatment, was given the new post of Chief of Planning and Development. His job is to make new proposals and to get them thoroughly discussed in every prison and among top and middle echelon policy makers. As Chief of Planning and Development he has no major operating responsibilities. His job is to anticipate innovations, prepare plans for formal consideration and turn over their implementation to an operating staff.

A non-governmental *Institute for the Study of Crime and Delinquency* was established at Berkeley to conduct basic research that would be less appropriately sponsored by California's correctional agencies. Richard A. McGee, Director of Corrections, is its President, and Heman G. Stark, Director of the Department of the Youth Authority, the Vice President. All but one of its other five Board members are or have been responsible for operational research in the correctional field.[1] The Institute staff began with making an international survey of practices and research in North America and Europe. This research program reflects awareness of the fact that correctional reform is an international cause. Much can be learned from the study of countries in which correctional work is done without the limits imposed by American legal and social traditions. The search is on for ideas with promise wherever they may be found.

The opportunity for making innovative suggestions is not restricted to these special posts. It has been decentralized and includes the previously mentioned Research Department, with its more than forty staff members. All of them are expected to look at data related to correctional operations and to interpret them from the point of view of what can be learned to improve correctional procedures. Not only at the top echelon of prison administration, but at the institutional level, employees have opportunities for trying out a new idea. Looking forward to the future is not a monopoly of any one man or any one organizational unit.

As new reform ideas emerge, the old ones do not disappear. They are submerged for a time in the "favorite child" approach which administrators resort to in order to start something new that has not yet proved to be illusory and, therefore, can be thought to

---

1J. Douglas Grant, Director of Research, Department of Corrections; Keith Griffith, Director of Research, Department of the Youth Authority; Milton Burdman, Chief of Planning and Development, Department of Corrections; Emmett Daly, Member, Youth Authority and formerly an Assistant Attorney General in charge of all research sponsored by the Attorney General; John V. Lemmon, the only person not employed by a state correctional agency, is an attorney enlisted to conduct the Institution's business affairs.

have promise. It is not surprising that within the Department of Corrections one finds support for nearly all of the reformation programs that have emerged in the recent history of the correctional movement. As in any social-psychological treatment field, where final answers are not available, correction officials responsible for planning are reluctant to give up any technique that looks plausible.

The clergy, who hope to inspire and convert inmates to goodness and who, at one time, dominated the correctional reform movement, are still represented. Prisons are among the few state agencies in which ministers serve as paid state employees. Work, vocational, and academic education have not diminished in value as a result of the organizational emphasis on therapeutically oriented treatment. Educational intervention enjoys a high degree of acceptance as a change mechanism within the organization and the general public.

Competition among the advocates of these various reform programs has been subdued. All of them were co-opted to support group counseling and milieu treatment, for none are excluded from taking part in it. They can play as large a role as they want to assume. There also is the fact that the Department as a whole is expanding. Employees need not be worried about losing their jobs as new ideas are introduced requiring new types of staff members. On the contrary, expansion may open up new routes for promotion and organizational mobility. An experimental approach to reform is more likely to be rewarded than censored, provided the new ideas are presented through appropriate administrative channels. This fact is perceived by many as evidence of being part of a "dynamic organization." The California system has grown for two decades and will keep on growing because the State's prison population is growing. Most Department of Corrections employees have advanced in income and social stature. They are part of an organization which has won high esteem both in the State and the country as a whole. While there is no shortage of "organization men" whose concern for their work does not go much beyond their own career ambitions, there are many who work for more than their pay-checks. On each eight-hour shift and in every department of the many prisons, forestry camps and other segments of the Department, one can find employees who believe that their jobs provide more than a living. Their work is a cause that inspires their lives. They have a positive identification with correctional reform ideals. This kind of enthusiasm influences other employees, at least to the extent that widespread lip service is paid to correctional reform ideals.

The Department's effort to institutionalize innovation has its limits. The Department of Corrections is a bureaucracy, with a military structure, in which authority is exercised from the top down. It is built on the model of all large scale organizations in which diverse elements interact on the basis of rules that facilitate a predictable division of labor. There is uncertainty, particularly among lower echelon personnel, about how seriously they should take the Department's avowed policy of welcoming new suggestions. They are worried that their more immediate superiors might disapprove. The writer found a considerable difference between headquarters and operational staff in readiness to express a personal point of view. Line employees often confided ideas, coupled with a request that they not be identified with the proposals. Several correctional officers are reported to have dropped group counseling activities because of the thinly veiled opposition to the program by their immediate superior, a sergeant or lieutenant. But the degree of readiness to speak one's mind seemed to this writer to be unusually high, when compared to other bureaucratic and large-scale organizations which the writer has had an occasion to observe or to be part of.

Innovation and status quo are in an equilibrium in which the former enjoys more prestige than the latter. As long as this subcultural trend is encouraged administratively from the top down, it has a chance to survive in the face of the natural tendency of all bureaucracies to nurture overly cautious and conformist organization men.

Chapter 10

CONCLUSION

THE CORRECTIONAL REFORM MOVEMENT

Observers of contemporary history are likely to have a short perspective about both people and events. History cannot be written by collating newspaper headlines. But the facts at hand are consistent with the theory that correctional reform is a contemporary scientific social movement of professional prison administrators. They share an identifiable ideology and a continuous history. They conceive of themselves as working for a common cause. They meet at national and international congresses to discuss common problems. All over the world, even in countries renowned for condoning some of the cruelest malpractices, there are experiments with the humane control of certain deviants. They emerge in part because these countries have a different legal system and historical traditions from those in the United States. Their common concerns have a long line of antecedents that serve to explain the present and can give us clues for anticipating the future.

Prison systems tend to have a conservative orientation. They express society's ultimate effort to enforce its laws against those whose actions or thoughts deviate from it. There is little formal opportunity for initiating changes by persons at lower echelons of its rigid caste system. Formal authority is exercised from above. Those who make policy must be responsive to the pull of conflicting values in modern societies regarding what can be expected from their prisons. For instance, the risks of living under minimum custody conditions to give inmates a chance to try out their capacity for self-control are limited by the expectation of the community that no prisoner be allowed to escape. Yet as this study has shown, a dynamic and a change oriented milieu can be developed within such a conservative social structure, by an emphasis on humanistic, scientific and newistic values.

The actual powers of prison administrators are less absolute than their formal powers. Power is shared in part with the inmates, their informal social structure and subculture. The latter are not in harmony with reform objectives. Prisoners have the power to be cooperative or recalcitrant. They do much of the work to keep the institutions going. While inmates are generally in agreement with the intent of reformers to decrease tension and hostility in the prison atmosphere, many oppose the rationale behind humanistic policies: changing the inmate, so that he can live up to acceptable social expectations. Many prisoners are unenthusiastic or opposed to activities designed to bring about their resocialization.

Donald Clemmer estimated in 1958 that 40 per cent of the American prisons have changed little in basic organization, institutional programs, or prison milieu since 1940 when his book was first published. In contrast, in the remaining 60 per cent, Clemmer indicates that humanitarian ideas have been influential in bringing about administrative change.[1] California is one of the states in which humanitarianism and the treatment point of view have come to predominate the entire state prison system. Here an effort has been made to co-opt the inmates to share in the plans of policy makers to create a more therapeutic milieu in prisons.

The California penal reform program is not an isolated administrative effort. It epitomizes the ideology of the American correctional movement. For nearly a century it has relied on religion, on education, and, more recently, on psychiatry as means for influencing both inmates and their subculture.

Prisons are staffed by persons trained in many helping professions. Their structure differs from mental hospitals in that there is no occupation in prison that can claim exclusive jurisdiction to positions of leadership. Over the years of the correctional reform movement, religious leaders have made spasmodic attempts to save the inmates and their souls. While the clergy rarely has much administrative influence in prisons, they were for many decades the only major professional group concerned with penal reforms.

---

[1]Donald Clemmer: *The Prison Community*. New York, Rinehart, 1958.

Since 1900, the clergy have been joined by educators, who have been challenged by the complexity of re-educating adults who have fallen by the wayside. But the number of educators with a special concern for penal work has never been large. The field of education, as the ministry, placed low professional priority on the application of their theories behind prison walls. The same degree of disinterest can be observed today among therapists and related treatment specialists. About the applicability of the therapeutic points of view on remaking prisoners, there has been more talking than doing. Only in recent years has there been a growing number of demonstrations of the pertinency of the therapeutic orientation to the prison world. In addition, other schools of thought, particularly the sociologists, have had an impact on prison reform.

None of these disciplines and professions claims exclusive jurisdiction over "the field." The prison world and its objectives, the resocialization of the inmates, can be viewed as an arena where representatives of varied helping professions interact in an effort to deal with a very complex task: the remaking of deviants, and if remaking is thought to be unlikely, their effective control. As yet, little is known about the effectiveness of the various techniques that are employed. The uncertainty that exists in the prisons, about how to treat inmates, is only a special instance of a more general behavioral science problem. Psychiatrists, psychologists, social workers, educators, vocational teachers and other specialists working elsewhere, in mental hospitals, schools, social agencies and in private practice, also are in search for more efficient means of remaking men to live up to society's expectations.

California does not have a special type of correctional reform. Many of its practices and key staff members were first seasoned in the Federal Bureau of Prisons. But what makes California stand out among American correctional systems is the degree to which reform ideals have influenced the entire state correctional service. In California they have been translated into a viable program. A direct line of influence can be traced from Enoch Wines, the prime mover of the 1870 *Declaration of Principles* of the American Correctional Association, to Richard A. McGee who transformed them into the basis of a well functioning organization. It was no accident that he was also one of a committee of three who edited the extensive revision of these principles in 1960.[1]

Reform cannot be static. This truism is all the more apparent in California, a state with a rapidly expanding population. In spite of the fact that some modern facilities have been built since World War II, the Director of Corrections reported to the Governor in 1959 that "within a year capacities will be nearly 4,000 less than the inmate population." He pointed out that with continued overcrowding the problem of idleness among the inmates is becoming more acute.[2] The California prison population increased between 1944 and 1960 by nearly 400 per cent (see Chart 8). This rise occurred in spite of the fact that California has become increasingly more liberal in the application of parole and probation. The state's population has mushroomed since World War II. The Department also has to accept all persons sent to it by the courts because of conviction of a felony. It also takes care of older youths, wards of the Youth Authority, who are housed in one of the Department's training facilities. More prisons have to be built, or new programs developed, to reduce crime or to handle more criminals outside of prisons.

Correctional work is not an elective form of social service. The poor can and often are neglected. The consequences in higher disease, mortality, and unhappiness have often been ignored. Children can be under-educated. But the criminals cannot be ignored without great peril. But there can be difference in policy about what is to be done with them.

Correctional work involves many controversial issues about the exisiting social order. For instance, the United States leads the world in the volume of research on correctional problems. But it also has the highest per capita volume of recorded crime. Can a society that places great emphasis on material things expect to be without persons who use non-acceptable means to attain them? Are some of our crimes an inevitable by-product of the existence

---

[1]The committee consisted of Peter P. Lejins, Professor of Sociology, University of Maryland, Chairman; Benjamin Frank, Ph.D., Chief of Research and Statistics of the Federal Bureau of Prisons; and Richard A. McGee.

[2]California State Department of Corrections, *Biennial Report, 1957-1958*. Sacramento, California, February 1, 1959.

of contradictory social values? California's prisons are filled with drug addicts, who are not regarded as criminals in England. American laws are severe with homosexual deviants. Judges are often lenient with *White Collar* criminals. The victims of criminal acts are given little consideration. Those who perpetrate crimes are rarely required to provide restitution to those who have been hurt by the crimes. Hundreds of thousands of men are idle or only half employed in prisons and jails throughout the land, a fantastic waste of manpower resources and a detriment to the morale of many of the inmates.

Correctional administrators as individuals tend to be cautious in their public pronouncements policy on controversies that have a bearing on these questions. But they help to keep them before the general public through the correctional movement and its organized activities. Its national and international character makes it easier to call attention to procedures elsewhere where some of these problems are being dealt with imagination and promise.

SCIENCE AND THE SOCIAL MOVEMENT

The correctional movement must be differentiated from political and religious social movements. Like Protestantism, Temperance, Communism, Christian Science, National Socialism, and Social Credit, correctional reform represents an organized effort to bring about a change. But unlike these non-scientific movements, the correctional movement has been influenced heavily by scientific principles. John Howard, Enoch C. Wines and more contemporary leaders have been important as exponents and administrators of a program. They never became deified. Correctional reforms always involve matters of conviction, but their acceptance is also related to hope that innovations might contribute to the attainment of the movement's objectives. Few penologists would view any innovation as so sacred that it could not be challenged by data indicating the failure of a practice to accomplish the objective for which it is pursued. Conversely, evidence supporting a practice would greatly strengthen it. Factors such as the personality of leaders, the ideological precepts of the movement, and economic, social and power considerations have played subsidiary roles in determining the course of the correctional movement.

The ascendancy of science in that movement is well illustrated in the 1960 revision of the *Declaration of Principles* of the American Correctional Association. While many of the humane sentiments first enunciated by Enoch Cobb Wines and his contemporaries were retained, Principle No. I states:

> The prevention and control of crime and delinquency are urgent challenges to the social sciences. The growing body of scientific knowledge, coupled with the practical wisdom and skill of those professionally engaged in society's struggle with the problem of criminality, provides the soundest basis for effective action.[1]

The 1960 revision introduces a new tone, a new language, and many new ideas. Like the earlier versions, it is still "ahead" of contemporary practice. Neither the policies of the Federal Bureau of Prisons nor the Department of Corrections of the State of California live up to all of its stipulations. The Declaration presents goals to be achieved and does not restrict itself to already demonstrated accomplishments.

THE EFFECTIVENESS OF REFORM

For over eighteen years California has been the site of a well planned and stable administrative effort to control the prison subculture and help to resocialize the inmates. The extent to which the California Department of Corrections has succeeded in attaining this objective is only partially answered by our findings. We know that its present staff verbalizes many reform attitudes. It participates actively in the Department's reform program. It includes many well educated and professionally trained employees.

But, are these staff intentions influencing the prisoners? We do not have questionnaire data on what the inmates think of the Department's treatment approach. But it is known that they participate in large numbers. Those who were involved in group counseling did "their time" peacefully. They committed fewer violations of prison rules than inmates who took no interest in

---

[1]Declaration of Principles of the American Correctional Association, 1960 revision, *American Journal of Correction*, September-October, 1960, Vol. 22, No. 5.

STAFFING AND COST PATTERNS– 1944–1960
DEPARTMENT OF CORRECTIONS, STATE OF CALIFORNIA

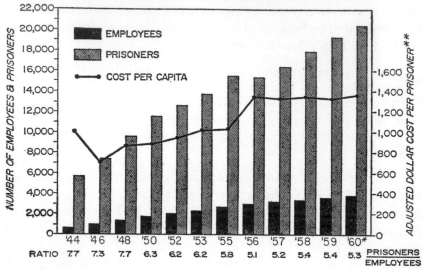

RATIO	7.7	7.3	7.7	6.3	6.2	6.2	5.8	5.1	5.2	5.4	5.4	5.3	PRISONERS / EMPLOYEES

*BASED ON DATA AS OF JUNE 30, EACH YEAR

CHART 8

group counseling or those who had been on a waiting list because of a shortage of group leaders and space for group meetings.

But is the existence of a program sufficient evidence of its effectiveness? Obviously not. Nor can there be a single criterion for a program of correctional systems that aims to accomplish several things. In days gone by, the most important criteria were: low cost to taxpayers and satisfying the politicians. Among contemporary professional leaders of the correctional movement other criteria predominate:

1. Are prisons safe for both inmates and their staff and are violations contained within reasonable bounds?

2. Can most inmates be released on parole before their sentences expire without added risk to public safety?

3. Are prisons able to attract and keep personnel who are adequately trained to perform their jobs?

4. Can the staff work together without disabling jurisdictional conflicts within the Department?

5. Is the prison system primarily concerned with the task of

controlling and treating its inmates rather than being utilized for political purposes?

6. Has a treatment program been developed that contributes to the adjustment of inmates to prison life?

7. Is there awareness within the organization that crucial problems are far from being resolved? Are administrative efforts being made to resolve them?

These goals have been achieved to a considerable extent in the California Department of Corrections. One key criterion for measuring correctional effectiveness, however, is far from being reached.

8. Does imprisonment in general or a particular technique of treatment contribute to the permanent rehabilitation of offenders as good citizens?

There is evidence that prison treatment is related to a reduction of prison rule violations. It seems to help inmates to accept prison restrictions. But the impact of various treatment procedures on recidivism is more a matter of conjecture. The bulk of all prison inmates continues to be people who have been in other prisons and jails.

There has been an improvement since the department has been organized in 1944, if penal reform is to be measured by the resources that have been mobilized to bring about change. The ratio of staff to inmates, as shown in Chart 8, has been reduced. More and better trained personnel are available to work with inmates. But if their often dedicated efforts are to be evaluated by its outcome, the question of progress cannot be answered. We know, as yet, little which reform programs have what kind of an impact on the various categories of inmates, nor do we know very much about the more or less untreatable cases.

The Department of Corrections is aware of these gaps in knowledge. Unlike many comparable organizations, it is officially concerned with collecting data that will provide evidence that would clarify unsolved questions of the social practice professions. In prisons, as in all applied social science fields, conclusive answers exist for only a very few practices. The correctional practitioner who accepts the theory that he must use science in decision making has little to work with; he is like a man who has learned to read, but his primer is filled with chapters lacking a conclusion and many blank pages.

And when the practitioner has evidence, he cannot always use it. Detailed clinical studies are made at the Reception-Guidance Centers of each man as he enters the prison system. But in spite of improvements in the quantity and technical quality of prison employees, the staff is insufficient to make full use of each case study.

The Department has not been able to decentralize its larger institutions. The Legislature has not supported the request to expand by building many independent small units. Budget analysts have been more concerned with the efficiency of having one large kitchen, laundry, and heating unit for a prison city than the human relations advantages of having several small more intimate institutions. When sites for prisons were proposed, residents opposed the idea of a prison being built nearby. As a result, much of the expansion of facilities was on sites already owned by state correctional departments, in spite of evidence that large institutions develop an over-complex bureaucratic structure and a milieu of impersonality.

Administrative and political considerations have to be weighed along with scientific ones. And above all, few decisions can wait for a thorough study of pertinent evidence. It takes more than intent to apply science to practice. It takes personnel, and money. The Department has more of both than before 1944, but not enough to keep up with its own professional standards.

Group Treatment: An Illustration of Policy Formation

The program of the Department of Corrections, including its group treatment emphasis, exists in a prison system in which many of the employees express pride. Prison walls are not used to hide practices that would be repugnant to public opinion. There is a widely shared awareness of the fact that prisons have to perform an important social function, within a network of often conflicting public, staff, and inmate expectations. There is concern with finding new ways of solving age old problems. Findings of criminological research are quickly disseminated among policy makers and some line personnel.

A significant minority of the employees embraced group treatment with a greater personal investment than would be true of routine administrative instructions. As a result, top correctional administrators could place increasing reliance on this form of prisoner-correctional employee interaction. It was advocated as something more than a technique. It also embodied the hopes of many as a progressive step in the corrections field.

Short of making a comprehensive social anthropological survey of Departmental personnel and their morale, the roots of this enthusiasm can only be surmised on an ex-post facto basis. The writer's observations lead him to conclude that the group treatment idea generally, and group counseling in particular, served a number of functions important to the Department of Corrections and its mission:

1. *Treatment Function.* Prescribed group interaction is primarily thought of as a mechanism by which correctional employees can reach a large number of inmates in what is organizationally defined as "treatment." Many policy makers and other employees expressed the view that even if group treatment did little to bring about fundamental personality change, group programs help inmates to become more accessible to other types of treatment. They provide an avenue for officials and inmates to get to know one another and develop some common ground in shared therapeutic objectives and experiences.

2. *Reassurance Function.* Recipes are quite varied for dealing with the social and psychological troubles of inmates. Our state of knowledge falls short of providing a confidence-inspiring basis for deciding among several plausible, alternate methods of inmate management.

Employees expected to perform a job under such circumstances want to believe that there are "solutions." Group treatment provides the basis of hope that there is one. It is advocated as a technique to reform inmates during their incarceration. Confidence in this possibility is enhanced by the attribute of newism and the sanctioning of group treatment by a scientific social movement. The enthusiastic support derived from this fact provides reassurance both to the correctional officers and the inmates, both of whom stand to gain from participating in group counseling. The program is a focus of mutual interest in an authoritarian system that otherwise differentiates sharply between free and inmate personnel. When such shared enthusiasm can be aroused, and to the extent that it can be maintained, the participants are helped to sustain a belief that it provides motivation to the inmate to change.

This belief, irrespective of whether it is warranted, facilitates integration to alternate, but frequently contradictory requirements, of the work life of penal employees. They are expected to insure effective custody of prisoners while individualizing their management. Newism and social movements are an antidote to boredom and retreatism[1] likely to arise among employees expected to live up to the contradictory expectations which the public has of its prisons.

3. *Achievement Function*. Group treatment is within the capacity of most employees, including lower echelon custody officials. Hitherto the latter were unable to participate in the system's most highly prized and rewarded goal: treatment. Group counseling provided more than one-third of the non-clinically trained personnel with institutionally acceptable means to achieve an objective formerly only within reach of professional personnel who had been employed for the exclusive purpose of providing treatment.

4. *Education Function*. Group treatment leaders in the Department of Corrections learn to look at imprisonment from the inmate point of view. It provides them with occasions for enhancing their understanding of how prisoners think and feel. Such knowledge heightens the capacity for empathy and insight of both group leaders and inmates.

5. *Experimentation Function*. Espousal of the group treatment idea by a segment of enthusiastic employees facilitated the program's technical development. The program grew big enough

---

[1]The contradictory expectations of persons working in prisons are conducive in some employees to a reaction of negating both the treatment and custody objectives and denying their meaningfulness. Their approach to work is one of indifference other than the performance of duties that is minimally required to get a pay check. Robert K. Merton designates this type of reaction as *retreatism*. See Robert K. Merton, *Social Theory and Social Structure*. Glencoe, Illinois, The Free Press, 1957.

to become a "laboratory" for testing its assumptions and beliefs. New methods must always be tried before one gathers data to test them.

6. *Morale Function.* A scientific social reform movement generally enhances the morale and prestige of the individuals and the organization associated with it. Its distinctive, novel elements are pregnant with the possibility of substantive scientific discovery. Many of its leaders and inmate clients have invested emotion in the idea. The activity tends to be watched with interest by administrators in their professional reference group. It makes every worker a "special case" and every client someone receiving personalized attention.[1] Newspaper reporters are always ready to observe something new and call it to the public's attention. Participation in a new program transforms what may have been "just a job" into something very exciting and full of discovery and creativity. Thus, it contributes to organizational morale and prestige.

7. *Integrative Function.* Prisons, in common with all total institutions, have a rigid caste line between those who manage and those who are managed. The autocratic element is particularly prone to be stressed because degradation, or loss of social status, is one of the main reasons for sending men to prison.[2] Status barriers, however, also inhibit communcation between the inmates who need to reform and the staff hired to help them reform.

The Department of Corrections has used group counseling as a vehicle to counteract the communication barriers inherent in any caste system. Through these groups, most of the inmates and a large minority of the staff interact to discuss common problems.

8. *Professionalization Function.* Group treatment has facilitated a highly prized goal: the professionalization of correctional work.[3] This trend enhances both the status of the worker and the

---

[1]Alfred H. Stanton and Morris S. Schwartz point out that the special case idea serves a variety of therapeutic functions. "Cases come to feel more like individuals; therapeutic workers more like unique instruments whose efforts make a difference because they are particularized to meet specific circumstances, usually viewed as being 'unusual.'" Alfred H. Stanton and Morris S. Schwartz, "The Problem of the Special Case," *The Mental Hospital,* New York, Basic Books, 1954.

[2]Norman A. Polansky: "The Prison as an Autocracy," *Journal of Criminal Law and Criminology,* Vol. 33, May-June, 1942.

[3]Lloyd E. Ohlin, Herman Piven and Donnel M. Poppenforth: "Major Dilemmas

work he does. Many employees have supplemented their counseling by the taking of relevant courses and the reading of books. As professionalization proceeds, the prestige of the field grows. This gives attention to persons within it. Also, larger numbers of technically skilled people can be attracted to make a career in the correctional field.

These eight functions do not carry equal weight with administrators. Group interactions have been primarily justified because of their imputed treatment potential. But the acceptance of this program by staff members was re-enforced by the other somewhat less publicly acknowledged functions—reassurance, achievement, education, experimentation, morale, integration and professionalization. Even in the absence of strong evidence that group counseling brings about basic reforms in the personality and social adjustment of prisoners after their release, these more latent functions help to explain why there is so much organizational enthusiasm for the program.

It does not matter, too, that group counseling falls very much short of being a *proved* remedy for prison problems. In penology, as in all helping professions, practices can be advocated on the basis of several alternative reasons:

1. Evidence that a technique helps.
2. Plausible reasons that a technique could help, without confirmatory evidence.
3. Lack of confidence in alternative technique as having greater plausibility for being effective than the technique of first preference.
4. Absence of evidence that a technique is harmful.

All four types of justification can be used to support the continuation and expansion of existing correctional programs, of group treatment as well as of its alternate techniques, such as vocational education, academic education, incarceration, and loss of civil rights. The newism theory could explain why one of these tech-

---

of the Social Worker in Probation and Parole," *The National Probation and Parole Association Journal*, Vol. 3, July, 1956; also Donald R. Cressey, "Professional Correctional Work and Professional Work in Correction," *The National Probation and Parole Association Journal*, Vol. 5, January, 1959.

niques has been singled out for special organizational attention. The element of innovation supported officials to make their best guess and to believe that it is a trustworthy answer to their operational problems. This belief has given them confidence to act. Acceptance of group treatment as "worth trying" was facilitated by the common sense process of substitution of social reassurance for as an yet unavailable scientific data. But if evidence were to turn up that the idea does not work as well as had been anticipated, a scientific movement is usually ready to espouse still newer ideas. Organizational flexibility is encouraged in this way: rigidity and lethargy towards the inmates are discouraged.

Newism is thus antithetical to the predisposition in any group, and particularly in bureaucratic organizations, to stabilize traditional relationships. Within a newistic philosophy, it becomes more difficult for persons to defend vested interests from the demand that alternate ways of getting the job done be considered. Newism functions as an antidote to organizational ritualism, but it also provokes anxiety in persons who do not feel adequate to the task assigned to them. They have difficulty enough to meet existing work standards. They prefer to organize their job so that there always is a standard operating procedure for problems with which they are confronted.

Group treatment has not become the creed of a new cult. The Department's leadership has been able to distinguish between the hope that could be entertained that group treatment is adding to the Department's capability; and unwarranted confidence that the program, by its sheer existence, is actually accomplishing this objective. In no field of endeavor, and certainly not in prison work, have experts found a panacea. Yet they must act. Were they to fail to act because all the desired evidence is not available, responsibility for action would probably go to persons less knowledgeable and more willing to make exaggerated and dishonest claims. Scientific social movements, such as the one described, coordinate the scientific point of view with the pragmatic orientation of administration.

THE SCIENTIFIC SOCIAL MOVEMENT THEORY

The correctional movement serves to illustrate a pattern of planned social change that warrants being examined for the generalizations which it suggests. Documentation of the validity of this theory cannot be undertaken within the framework of this study. It would require the making of systematic analyses of other scientific social movements. The theory's plausibility will, however, be apparent to many who are acquainted with the history of some psychosocial treatment schools of thought. There is, for instance, Freudian psychoanalysis which is having a significant influence on the correctional movement. The charismatic leadership of its founder has given way to a well developed organizational framework, led by men dedicated to the objective of advancing the movement's influence. The ideas of Sigmund Freud remain accepted as gospel by segments of the movement that call themselves "orthodox," but they are being modified by new evidence as well as new, as yet unproved hunches, of "neo-Freudian" schools of thought.

Psychoanalysis has no parallel social action program like that formulated by the correctional movement, but it has pursued consciously the objective of presenting its point of view through the organization of professional adherents. They meet periodically in national and international conventions. Ernest Jones describes how he proposed to Freud the formation of "a small group of trustworthy analysts as a sort of 'Old Guard' around Freud. It would give him the assurance that only a stable body of firm friends could. It would be a comfort in the event of further dissensions, and it should be possible for us to be of practical assistance by replying to criticism and providing him with necessary literature, illustrations for his work drawn from our own experience, and the like. There would be only one definite obligation undertaken by us: namely, that if anyone wishes to depart from any of the fundamental tenets of psychoanalytical theory, e.g., the conception of repression, of the unconscious, of infantile sexuality, etc., he would promise not to do so publicly before first discussing his views with the rest."[1]

---

[1]Ernest Jones: *The Life and Work of Sigmund Freud. New York,* Basic Books, 1955, Vol. 2. On May 25, 1913 when the Committee first assembled as a whole, Freud celebrated the event by presenting each member with an antique Greek intaglio from his collection which they then got mounted in a gold ring. Freud himself had long carried such a ring.

Freud himself was enthusiastic and wrote to Jones: "What took hold of my imagination immediately is your idea of a secret council of the best and most trustworthy among our men to take care of the further development of psychoanalysts and defend the cause against personalities and accidents when I am no more."

Psychoanalysis has many newistic elements. It is rooted in science, but many of its inferences were then and still are highly speculative. The latter survive by being avowed like articles of faith, perpetuated by devoted followers and challenged by rebellious competitors like Otto Rank, Carl Jung, and Alfred Adler, who wanted to head their own psychoanalytic movement. The psychoanalytic movement developed a clearly defined status system, a mechanism for perpetuating itself through training and indoctrination and through organizations such as psychoanalytic institutes and the American Psychoanalytic Society.

CAN PLANNED CHANGE BE INSTITUTIONALIZED?

Administrative support of group treatment discouraged the kind of organized opposition which plagued the enthusiasts of psychoanalysis during their early years of striving for recognition. As a result, group counseling did not have to be defended militantly against professional prestige figures identified with alternate, and often equally unproven solutions. The personnel of the Department of Corrections were able to elaborate their group treatment program to the point where its assumptions can now be tested by scientific techniques rather than continue reliance on hope and faith.

This acceptance, in principle, of scientific discipline, makes a scientific social movement inherently unstable. Its rational orientation is opposed to bureaucratic routinization for the sake of more stability. However, the spirit of innovation, even when organizationally encouraged, has a precarious existence. It could be discouraged by fearful top-echelon administrators. A few years of budgetary stringency can destroy it. If the Department of Corrections were to stop expanding, if there were few raises in salary, few opportunities for promotion, and losses of the cadre of persons who are now enthusiastically identified with correctional reform, the

California Department of Corrections could return to the spirit
that prevailed in the 1930's, although it is doubtful that it will ever
again develop the structural forms under which all of the previous
inefficiencies and inequities could occur.

A subtle but growing obstacle to professional enthusiasm that
facilitates change is the growing size of the Department of Corrections. In 1944 when it was begun, the Director could personally
select key employees and work with them intimately to develop a
team spirit. It was possible to have personal knowledge of a good
many of the 746 employees on the payroll on June 30, 1944. But
with a payroll that has gone beyond 4,000 persons, a more administrative and less personal approach to staff selection has to be made.
Since the number of prisoners continues to increase, further increases in the size of the personnel and greater dispersion of correctional institutions throughout California can be expected. The
trend towards bigness is symbolized by the appointment of McGee
on October 1, 1961 to the post of Agency Administrator of all the
state's correctional agencies, including the Department of Corrections, the Department of the Youth Authority, the Adult Authority
(parole board), the Youth Authority (parole board), the Board of
the California Institution for Women, and other formerly autonomous or semi-autonomous correctional state boards. This kind of
centralization will make it easier to infuse reform policies throughout the entire corrections network. However, the possibility of
charismatic personal influence on the staff by the director is reduced
by the size of this bureaucratic establishment. It has to be expressed
through less personal and more administrative means.

The present Director of the Department has served in the
cabinet of three California governors of two different parties.
Nearly twenty years have passed since any serious effort has been
made to make political considerations primary in the Department's
management. Legislators and the governor's office have, in the past,
been kept well informed about the reform orientation of the Department. Prisons and prisoners are a central issue of public policy.
No correctional program can be sustained for long without social
and political support. But a new governor or legislature with policies that are quite contrary to those now employed in the Depart-

ment would quickly affect day-to-day operations. Any Director of the Department of Corrections serves at his Governor's pleasure. Similarly the Legislature through its power to make or withhold appropriations has an influence on what happens in the prison system.

THE CHALLENGE REMAINS

The organized correctional reform program, more than ninety years old, is approaching its centennial with evidence that it can be administratively implemented. Its humanistic ideals are being applied. Constitutional guarantees against cruel and unusual punishment are being kept. Rationality rather than emotion and revenge is the principal method for weighing alternate prison policies. Research is being undertaken to reduce the arena of uncertainty in correctional administration. Much has been learned about the etiology of crime, prisons as social systems, and the management of men under conditions of incarceration. But the reform movement has failed to solve a number of fundamental social welfare problems. Signor Scalia's statement at the first prison congress in 1870, reviewing conditions from 1820 to his time, bears being repeated. It is not yet outdated:

> For the last fifty years, the efficiency of the different penitentiary systems has been carefully debated, but that question has not yet made much progress; and, at present, as was the case a long time ago, the champions of different schools are ranged in the field of abstractions, to go over the same arguments, and to allege on both sides the same facts and experiments. Though chains have been broken, though corporeal punishment has been abolished, though the prisoner receives a better treatment than heretofore, though indulgence and leniency have now superseded the severity of punishment, nobody can tell me whether and how far this humanitarian spirit has stopped the corrupting current of guilt; what have been the effects of such or such other punishment; and none can inform me why they have deemed it better to be more lenient or more severe; and the problem about relapse still remains unsolved.[1]

[1]Signor Martino Beltrani Scalia: "Historical Sketch of National and International Penitentiary Conferences in Europe and America," *New York Prison Association, Twenty-sixth Annual Report.*

The incidence of crime is increasing, to the extent that official statistics can accurately measure criminal social deviancies. A disturbingly high proportion of prison inmates continue a life of crime, even after exposure to dedicated efforts to motivate them to reform their lives. Crime remains high on the agenda of society's unresolved crises. It is a problem that does not seem to decline as our technological capabilities increase. In 1961, a series of murders of inmates by fellow prisoners at San Quentin Prison highlighted the fact that many problems of inmate control remain. The correctional movement is conscious of these facts. Its scientific creed serves to facilitate the continued asking of questions and the search for new methods. It is possessed of a spirit of restlessness that counteracts the also well entrenched bureaucratic preference for achieving stability by settling for a publicly tolerable level of stagnation.

The correctional movement is poles apart in social prestige from other treatment movements, such as mental health, psychoanalysis, public health, and social work. The latter enjoy greater esteem. They also deal largely with clients who are more esteemed. They can count on better financial support to hire a larger proportion of trained personnel. But all of these helping professions, and the movements with which they are identified, share common questions about the effectiveness of their techniques. They use alternate routes of training and alternate as well as overlapping remedies for dealing with similar human problems.

These differences often are ignored by means of bureaucratic "cartel" agreements, in which each professional discipline is assigned a specified organizational role in return for acquiescence to a status quo sometimes dignified with the label of "The Team Approach." Such arrangements are standard operating procedures in child guidance clinics and mental hospitals. They serve to enhance the well-being of the professionals by removing such latent conflicts as would break out if there were too much emphasis on the fact that pyschiatrists have not yet demonstrated their claim to being most qualified in making psychiatric diagnostic judgments or in the administration of mental health facilities. A Master's degree in social work is no proof that the holder will turn in a superior performance in dealing with delinquents. Psychologists make extensive use of psychometric tests, the diagnostic utility of which is shrouded in much uncertainty.

In the prison work, a less limiting theory predominates: Training in some area is preferable to none at all. The helping professions work together with few organizationally-imposed prejudgments of their capabilities. No "cartel" agreement requires that a particular therapeutic role be carried on by persons of only one route of training. Prison work has not been sufficiently attractive as a jurisdiction to educators, social workers, psychologists, psychiatrists, and other professionals to become a major organizational target of any one of them. Each training specialty can use opportunities to demonstrate what it can accomplish, to the extent that trained personnel can be hired, and funds can be secured to pay them.

The co-existence of many psychosocial helping professions in the same treatment system gives the correctional field a significant potential as a research laboratory in comparative methods of treatment. In prisons it is, therefore, strategically possible to act on the recommendations of the Joint Commission on Illness and Mental Health that the jurisdictional uncertainties be dealt with primarily on the basis of evidence of "individual competence to undertake the given approach to a patient." The Commission recommends that "in the absence of more specific and definitive scientific evidence of causes of mental illness, psychiatry and the allied mental health professions should adopt and practice a broad, liberal philosophy of what constitutes and who can do treatment within the framework of their hospital or other professional service agencies. . . ."[1]

While there is uncertainty on how best to treat prisoners in order to reform them, the uncertainty should not be allowed to divert attention from the fact that criminologists know far more than administrators are able and willing to apply. Many of the fairly well validated findings cannot be implemented because of organizational barriers. There are doctrinaire obstacles to their

---

[1]Joint Commission on Illness and Mental Health: *Action for Mental Health, Final Report of Joint Commission on Illness and Mental Health.* New York, Basic Books Inc., 1961.

acceptance by administrators who feel more comfortable with existing practices as an article of faith rather than as a tentative scientific procedure. Since changes often cost money, the budgetary limits of correctional organizations also serve as a deterrent to the application of knowledge.

Research alone will not suffice. Opportunities for the application of findings must also be expanded. The correctional movement aims to support their development all over the country. It provides a cautious, but steady lever to influence a generally conservative public opinion to accept more readily than it has in the past experimentation in penology. Advances in knowledge in the social sciences have been greater than opportunities of application, that were politically acceptable. Crime control remains an area of public policy in which traditional and emotional expectations strongly influence what can be tried to resocialize criminals. The slow pace of change in correctional practices, when compared to the nearly century long steadiness in objectives, must be understood in this social context.

Appendix

DECLARATION OF PRINCIPLES OF THE AMERICAN CORRECTIONAL ASSOCIATION

as adopted by the American Congress of Correction
1960

The 90th Annual Congress of Correction of the American Correctional Association and the Editors of the *American Journal of Correction* on behalf of the members of the Association wish to express their deep appreciation for the long and arduous months of unselfish and competent labor spent by the Committee on the Revision of the Declaration of Principles which resulted in such a clear and enlightened statement of the Association's purposes and ideals. This is the first revision since 1930, and from a careful reading it may be doubted that any revision will be needed for a great many years.

Our sincerest thanks to Dr. Peter P. Lejins, Chairman, Richard A. McGee, and Dr. Benjamin Frank.

PREAMBLE

The American Congress of Correction, to reaffirm the basic ideals and aspirations of its membership, to encourage a more enlightened criminal justice in our society, to promote improved practices in the treatment of adult and juvenile offenders, and to rededicate its membership to the high purposes stated by its founding leaders in 1870, does adopt this revised Declaration of Principles.

Principle I. The prevention and control of crime and delinquency are urgent challenges to the social sciences. The growing body of scientific knowledge, coupled with the practical wisdom and skill of those professionally engaged in society's struggle with the problem of criminality, provide the soundest basis for effective action.

Principle II. The forces for the prevention and control of crime and delinquency ultimately must find their strength from the constructive qualities of the society itself. The properly functioning basic institutions—such as the family, the school and the church, as well as the economic and political institutions—and a society united in the pursuit of worthwhile goals are the best guarantees against crime and delinquency. The willingness of the society to maintain a rationally organized and properly financed system of corrections, directed toward the reclamation of criminals and juvenile delinquents, is a prerequisite of effective control.

Principle III. Both punishment and correction are at present our methods of preventing and controlling crime and delinquency. Further improvement and expansion of the correctional methods should be the generally accepted goal, fully in line with the spirit of the penal reform of the past century and our current correctional progress.

Principle IV. Traditionally, violators of the criminal law have been differentiated into those who are mentally sick and should be handled as such and those who are considered criminally responsible. The best legal and psychiatric knowledge should be employed to define this distinction.

Principle V. Until the guilt of the suspected offender has been established in the course of due process of law, he should be considered innocent and his rights as a free citizen should be respected, except for such restraints as are indispensable to insure the proper investigation and trial.

Principle VI. If, as a result of a miscarriage of justice, an individual has been made to suffer, he should receive reasonable indemnification.

Principle VII. The correctional facilities, comprising both institutional and non-institutional treatment—probation and parole—should be planned and organized as an integrated system under a central authority responsible for guiding, controlling, unifying and vitalizing the whole.

Principle VIII. The variety of treatment programs corresponding to the different needs of the offenders suggests a diversification of correctional institutions resulting in a system of specialized institutions so classified and coordinated and so organized in staff and program as to meet the needs of those offenders who present specific problems. The spirit of continued experimentation with new types of institutions and agencies which show promise of more effective results should be encouraged and supported.

Principle IX. Repeated short sentences imposed for recurring misdemeanors or petty offenses, are ineffective, both as means of correction and as a punitive deterrent. These sentences often are a contributing factor in the career of the petty recidivist. An integrated system of control by means of special institutional facilities and community supervision is essential for the solution of this problem. Further research and experimentation with agencies and institutions of other than the conventional type offer the greatest promise.

Principle X. The architecture and construction of penal and correction institutions should be functionally related to the programs to be carried on in them. The great variety of existing programs, to be further diversified in the future, indicates the need for a similar variety and flexibility of architectural design and type of construction. The building standards and technological advances of the day should be reflected in these institutions. The current skepticism about inordinately large institutions suggests the desirability of institutions of moderate size, which may be more costly to build and operate, but which lend themselves better to the fulfillment of the objectives of a good correctional institutional program.

Principle XI. The organization and administration of correctional institutions and agencies is one of the more complex areas of public administration and deals with one of the most involved of social problems. It is essential that the administration of the correctional agencies meet the highest standards of public administration and that all employees be selected in accordance with the best available criteria and serve on the basis of merit and tenure systems.

Principle XII. The special and complex problems characteristic of criminal and delinquent behavior imply the need for suitable personality traits and specialized skills on the part of the personnel and hence the need for special professional education and training of a high standard, including pre-service and continued in-service training.

Principle XIII. Correctional institutions and agencies can best achieve their goal of rehabilitation by focusing their attention and resources on the complete study and evaluation of the individual offender and by following a program of individualized treatment.

Principle XIV. The sentence or disposition determining the treatment for the offender should be based on a full consideration of the social and personality factors of the particular individual.

In the many jurisdictions these investigations may be made at different levels, so long as the essential information is available to the court or treatment authority at the time crucial case decisions are to be made.

Principle XV. A punitive sentence should properly be commensurate with the seriousness of the offense and the guilt of the offender. Inequality of such sentences for the same or similar crimes is always experienced as an injustice both by the offender and the society. On the other hand, the length of the correctional treatment given the offender for purposes of rehabilitation depends on the circumstances and characteristics of the particular offender and may have no relationship to the seriousness of the crime committed. In a correctionally oriented system of crime control, the indeterminate sentence administered by qualified personnel offers the best solution.

Principle XVI. The principles of humanity and human dignity to which we subscribe, as well as the purposes of rehabilitation require that the offenders while under the jurisdiction of the law enforcement and correctional agencies, be accorded the generally accepted standards of decent living and decent human relations.

Their food, clothing and shelter should not be allowed to fall below the generally accepted standards, and they should be afforded the conventional conveniences made possible by our technological progress. Their health needs—both physical and mental—should be met in accordance with the best medical standards. Recreation should be recognized as a wholesome element of normal life.

Principle XVII. Religion represents a rich resource in the moral and spiritual regeneration of mankind. Especially trained chaplains, religious instruction and counseling, together with adequate facilities for group worship of the inmate's own choice, are essential elements in the program of a correctional institution.

Principle XVIII. Rewards for conformance to the highest values of our culture should be given precedence over fear of punishment in guiding the development of human character in correctional systems as well as in society at large. Enlightened self-interest must be emphasized and made operative at all times.

Principle XIX. No law, procedure or system of correction should deprive any offender of the hope and the possibility of his ultimate return to full, responsible membership in society.

Principle XX. Moral forces, organized persuasion and scientific treatment should be relied upon in the control and management of offenders, with as little dependence upon physical force as possible.

Principle XXI. The task of evaluating the individual offender and developing the most appropriate treatment program must draw upon all the available knowledge and professional skill represented by sociology, psychology, psychiatry, social case work and related disciplines. Specialists and technicians from these fields must be welded into a diagnostic and treatment team by competent administrators, so that the disciplines they represent may become the core of the correctional treatment program.

Principle XXII. To assure the eventual restoration of the offender as an economically self-sustaining member of the community, the correctional program must make available to each inmate every opportunity to raise his educational level, improve his vocational competence and skills, and add to his information meaningful knowledge about the world and the society in which he must live.

Principle XXIII. To hold employable offenders in correctional institutions without the opportunity to engage in productive work is to violate one of the essential objectives of rehabilitation.

Without in any way exploiting the labor of involuntary confinees for financial gain, or unduly interfering with free enterprise, it is not only possible but imperative that all governmental jurisdictions give full cooperation to the establishment of productive work programs with a view to imparting acceptable work skills, habits, attitudes and work discipline.

Principle XXIV. Some of the criminal law violators who are found by the courts to be criminally responsible, but who are abnormal from the point of view of the modern disciplines of psychiatry and psychology, are in need of psychotherapy. Diagnostic and treatment facilities for such mentally abnormal offenders should be further developed at the appropriate stages of the correctional process.

Psychiatric and psychological services should be provided for the pre-sentence investigations of the courts; out-patient clinics for the use of the non-institutional treatment agencies—probation and parole; and psychiatric and psychological services within the penal and correctional institutions, even to the extent of developing special institutions for this type of offender.

Principle XXV. Recent research in the community aspects of the institutional populations suggests the importance of the group approach to the problem of correctional treatment. There is a need for more attention to the implications of this new method as well as the need to support and promote experiments and demonstration projects.

Principle XXVI. The exercise of executive clemency in the pardon of criminals is a question of great delicacy and difficulty. The use of this power should be limited largely to cases of wrongful conviction, or of excessive sentences constituting injustice, or, in rare instances, where extreme hardship is involved and executive dispensation is warranted. The practice of releasing large numbers of prisoners by executive clemency is generally condemned. The use of executive clemency or pardon to restore civil rights to a fully rehabilitated person who has established a record of responsible living for a period of years is, on the other hand, to be commended.

Principle XXVII. Suitable employment for a discharged or paroled offender is one of the major factors in his rehabilitation and the regaining of his lost position in society. The most forceful efforts and comprehensive methods should be exercised to secure such work. An understanding, favorable attitude and the participation of organized labor and management should be actively sought.

Principle XXVIII. Probation has come to be accepted as the most efficient and economical method of treatment for a great number of offenders. To enhance the achievement of the full potentialities of probation, mandatory exceptions to the use of probation with respect to specific crimes or to types of offenders should be eliminated from the statutes.

Current research indicates great possibilities for developing specific types and degrees of probationary supervision adapted to the needs of the individual offender.

Principle XXIX. With a few possible exceptions, all offenders released from correctional institutions should be released under parole supervision, and parole should be granted at the earliest date consistent with public safety and the needs of rehabilitation. Decisions pertaining to an individual's parole should be made by a professionally competent board. The type and degree of supervision should be adapted to the needs of the individual offender.

Principle XXX. The collection and publication of criminal statistics designed to provide information on the extent and nature of criminality and juvenile delinquency and on the various phases of the correctional process is indispensable for the understanding of crime and for the planning and evaluation of correctional and preventive measures.

Such statistics are necessary and should be developed on the national, state and local levels and should consist of statistics of the offenses known to the police, arrest statistics, judicial statistics, probation, institutional and parole statistics as well as criminal career records.

Principle XXXI. Research and the scientific study of the problems of juvenile delinquency and criminality and of the methods of dealing with these are essential prerequisites for progress. Through its educational, research and governmental institutions society should sponsor, finance and carry out both basic and applied research in this area. The law enforcement and correctional institutions and agencies should lend their support, take initiative and themselves engage in appropriate research as an indispensable part of their effort to improve their performance.

Principle XXXII. In a democracy the success of any public agency, including that of correctional institutions and agencies, depends in the final analysis on popular support. An adequate financial base, emphasis on the adequacy of personnel and, in general, insistence on an alert and progressive administration in corrections is the responsibility of the public and a function of its enlightened concern with crime and delinquency problems.

Principle XXXIII. The correctional process has as its aim the re-incorporation of the offender into the society as a normal citizen. In the course of non-institutional treatment the offender continues as a member of the conventional community. In the course of his institutional stay constructive community contacts should be encouraged. The success of the correctional process in all its stages can be greatly enhanced by energetic, resourceful and organized citizen participation.

INDEX

Adler, Alfred: 195
Adler, Mortimer J.: 74
American Correctional Association: 15,
 21; Declaration of Principles (1960):
 182-183, 185
American Correctional Association. *See
 also,* American Prison Association
 and National Prison Association
American Law Institute—Committee on
 Criminal Justice: 79
American Prison Association: 13-14, 15,
 17
American Social Science Association: 10
Auburn System: 8
Ayers, E. E.: xiii

Bailey, Walter C.: xiii; quoted: 172-173
Bates, Sanford: 73, 85
Beatty, Ronald: xii
Beaumont, August de: 3
Beccaria, Cesare Bonesana: 4
Bennett, James V.: xiii, 73, 85, 87
Bentham, Jeremy: 4
Boston Prison Discipline Society: 8
Bradford, William: 6-7
Brawley, E.: xiii
Briggs, Dennie L.: 171
Brockway, Zebulon: 12
Burdman, Milton: xii, 176-177; quoted:
 42

California Board of Prison Directors:
 81-82
California Bureau for Juvenile Research:
 78-79
California Bureau of Criminal Statistics—
 research: 137
California Department of Corrections—
 Board Study Commission: 128; Coordinator of Group Counseling: 158-

159; education of staff: 96-102; establishment: 60-61, 70, 85-90; evaluation
of group treatment programs: 163-
167; family counseling program: 169-
170; group counseling program: 42-
43, 48-58, 158-162; group psychotherapy program: 49, 143-156; group
treatment program (criticisms of):
172-173; group treatment program
(functions of): 188-192; growth: 196;
Halfway Houses: 176; Increased Correctional Effectiveness program: 173-
174; Inmate Advisory Councils: 120,
128-129; Institutional Classification
Committee: 117; milieu treatment
program: 170-175; personnel policies:
102-115, 119; Planning and Development: 176-177; Pre-Release Living
Units: 175-176; prison population
statistics: 46, 183; Reception Guidance Center: 117, 124; re-organiza-
tion 94-115; research: 137-140, 176-
178; Research Division: 48, 177; Special Adjustment Centers: 124-125;
Special Intensive Parole Unit: 92,
130-131, 174-175; staff: 46-47, 94-115;
staff attitudes toward group treatment programs: 153-156; staff attitudes toward jobs: 109-115; staff attitudes toward punishment: 27-33, 133-
136; staff attitudes toward research:
167-168; treatment programs: 124-141
California Director of Corrections: 83
California Federation of Women's Clubs:
 80
California Governor's Study Commission:
 137
California Institution for Men, Chino: 32,
 81-82, 95

209